PRAISE FOR *EMBRACE DIFFERENCE AND CHANGE THE WORLD*

'This book takes Diversity, Equity & Inclusion to another level beyond the traditional thinking in a very pragmatic and relatable way. Spending time to read your book has had a powerful impact on me and challenged the way I see the world, both inside and outside of the workplace! I found myself stopping and reflecting on recent situations and how I might respond differently in the future.'

Jon Summerson, Director of Culture and Organisational Development at the Royal British Legion

'This book is a great resource for anyone who has limited or no personal first-hand experience with neurodiversity and is interested to learn more. It is also a great source of information for leaders, educators and coaches as it is a wonderful reference guide and a guiding light for those seeking to truly embrace the challenge of building an inclusive society regardless of their occupation.'

Marina Polyakova, Global HR Director at ITW

'Thank you for your wonderful book. It was really easy to read with great links to embracing differences brought to life through storytelling. My thoughts are it will help leaders navigate their way through the complexity of managing people, especially since Covid, as well as help teachers and parents/grandparents understand how best to support their child/grandchild with complex needs. Your book is full of tips and exercises to build confidence around a complex subject. A handy book that you can refer back to as you move through different stages in your life.'

Julie Scorer, Leader at Lloyds Bank

'Any parent or relative of a neurodiverse child will find this book really useful and informative as well as reassuring that there's a reason for their child's behaviour. I personally found some of the exercises really useful and you've made the explanations very simple so they are accessible for all.'

Laura Chappell, CEO at
Brunel Pension Partnership Limited

'The book is SUPER. The tone is clear, human, guiding. I will do more of the exercises over time and I can imagine recommending it to clients. I think coaches will find it useful. Well done!!'

Remi Baker, CEO at Wondrous

'In this world marked by divisions, *Embrace Difference and Change the World* stands out as a beaming light of wisdom, offering an exploration of the transformative power inherent in embracing difference and understanding others. Sarah navigates the complex terrain of diversity, urging readers to dismantle preconceived ideas or views and build bridges of connection across varied perspectives.

'The strength of the book lies in its ability to weave together personal narratives, insights, and psychological perspectives, creating a map that underscores the importance of empathy. Sarah argues that embracing difference is not merely a social obligation but a deeply enriching journey that expands our own understanding of the world.

'One of the book's strengths is its approach to diversity. Rather than presenting a one-size-fits-all solution, Sarah acknowledges the complexity of human experiences and encourages readers to engage in active listening and open-minded exploration. Through engaging real-life examples, Sarah illustrates the profound impact that understanding others can have on fostering genuine connections.

'Sarah simply and skilfully addresses the barriers that often hinder us, such as cultural stereotypes, fear of the unknown, and the tendency to view differences as threats. By unpacking these obstacles, *Embrace Difference and Change the World* becomes a guide for readers seeking to move from their comfort levels and grow a genuine appreciation for the richness that diversity brings to our lives.

'Importantly, the book provides practical tools and exercises for readers to apply in their daily lives. Whether navigating workplace dynamics, fostering inclusivity in communities, or simply fostering meaningful conversations with friends and family, Sarah equips readers with actionable insights that empower them to foster positive change.'

Rob Dier, Franchise Director at Lookers

Embrace Difference
AND CHANGE THE WORLD

Sarah Lane

Embrace Difference and Change the World

Cover Design & Illustrations: Neil Coe
Typesetting: Neil Coe
Editing: Matthew Keeler
Proofreading: Victoria Denne

First Edition: 2024
ISBN: 978-1-0686-4791-8

Published with the support of Brandspire Digital Limited, United Kingdom
https://brandspire.co.uk

Printed in the United Kingdom

DEDICATION

To my wonderful family Marcus and Nick, my gratitude for your love and the gift of seeing the world through your differing eyes is unending. May the giggles and the tears keep us resilient, loving and connected for evermore.

ACKNOWLEDGEMENTS

Without the bumps in the road, I would not have been driven to write this book. The sheer anger, frustration and exhaustion caused when you meet up against roadblocks that make no sense turned into a real driver for me. Amongst them is the 18-month fight with children's social services, following three school breakdowns from age five to ten, to get our son access to appropriate specialist education, which left me with both a real sadness at how broken and inhumane the system has become and also hugely grateful for the resources I am blessed with to have the strength to navigate it. Not everyone has the blessing of a support network, financial stability, the education or tenacity to keep pushing, even when those in power say no.

So here I would like to pay tribute to and acknowledge those who, through my career and life, have been allies and advocates, as well as those who have been my rock, sounding board and shoulder to cry on (or scream over) when things have been really tough.

Firstly, I'll start at home with my wonderful, generous and ever-faithful husband Marcus. When we first got together 27 years ago, we realised we held the shared belief that true love is the total commitment to the full growth and development of the other. It's a belief that holds true today and serves us well as a family. My dear friends Sally and Jenny have been constants over the last 15 years in an ever-changing landscape. Your ability to truly listen and come from a place of non-judgement is a special gift to the world that I feel privileged to be able to access (often at odd hours, which I'm especially grateful for).

So many other people have been inspirations and guides through my journey. I know I cannot list them all, so here's at least a beginning: Kathryn, Claire, Carly, Lynn, Alastair, Patrizia, Mike, Phil, Ian, Fergal, Nicole, Wendy, Sarah-Jane, and so many more who have inspired me from afar. Huge thanks to you all.

INTRODUCTION

As the adoptive mother of an autistic ADHDer son, the wife of a neurodiverse husband and a working woman whose career so far spans three decades, I have focused in this book on the differences that I live and breathe. While you read this book, know that, although I am sharing stories and views based on gender and neurodivergence, I believe all differences are to be embraced. It's because I believe that it's important to NOT speak for others but to authentically speak from your own place in the system that these areas are my golden thread. I believe that if one minority group creates greater inclusion then the positive impact on the world will be felt by all.

Throughout the book, you will find personal stories from my life and my work with clients that I hope bring things into focus for you. Within these stories, I have changed the names of the individuals and have not referenced specific organisations. This is to protect the confidentiality that is so important in coaching and building psychologically safe environments where change can happen. I hope my use of personal references and stories brings the more technical or psychological aspects to life.

As you begin to read, know that this topic is one that will most likely call up memories, emotions and passions in you that, while welcome, can take time to process. To that end, allow yourself space for reflection, especially after taking part in any of the exercises or techniques offered in these pages. Remember also that change of any depth happens over time. We are multifaceted as human beings and so need time, space and energy to create sustainable change that happens 'in the muscle'. Although my hope as you read is that you learn more on this topic, my biggest wish is that together we can begin a ripple effect that will be felt through the generations, felt throughout our communities, our organisations, our families and our school systems, reaching beyond the cognitive and striving to be brave and sit with discomfort, inevitably getting things wrong but always working towards learning, growing and connecting.

CONTENTS

EXERCISE & TIPS INDEX

CHOICES BOOK

Check out my other book, Choices: From Confusion To Clarity, at
coachinglane.com/my-books/choices-from-confusion-to-clarity
or scan the QR code

FURTHER RESOURCES

To access further resources, and worksheets and stay
updated, go to the books' website page at
coachinglane.com/my-books/embrace-difference-change-the-world
or scan the QR code

CHAPTER 1

You can change the daily narrative and create equity

One of the few truths in this world is that we have a choice as to the stories we tell ourselves and others. Much of the narrative that is out in the world is outside of our control. However, we can filter it to make sure what we hear and say matches the world we want to live in. During the pandemic, many people I know stopped watching the news, outside of the 6pm daily briefing, because the reporting was so negatively framed that it was having an unintended impact on their mental health. The stories we tell and the ones we hear have far-reaching effects, so choosing what input you take and output you give has to be a priority.

We all have an inner voice, and what it says sets our behaviour

Before you start thinking to yourself, 'What is this woman on about? Inner voices, pish!', know that the voice saying that to you is the very voice that I am talking about here. The inner dialogue we have is something that is an inherent part of being human and, for some, may even be so vocal that it has a bigger 'airtime' than their actual voice in the outer world.

The voice and how we speak to ourselves impact more than just our thinking. The narrative we run and the tone of voice we use affect our physiology, our emotions and ultimately how we choose to live our lives. There's a lot at stake so it is worth exploring, understanding your own internal narrative and making any changes that are needed to affect your mind and your body. Change the chat and affect your behaviours.

Many cultures over thousands of years have known about the mind–body connection and in literal terms we experience this each moment of the day. This has been confirmed by researchers who have been able to map what happens when an external event occurs. Our brains take the data in and create an internal representation of the experience. This internal representation affects our state/feelings (positive or negative) and also our physiology/body. These three elements are all linked and affect one another interdependently.

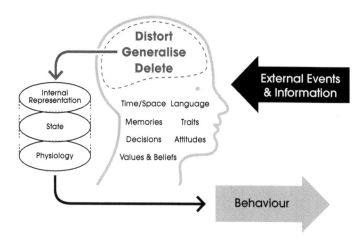

In the last decade alone, I have tested this connection explicitly during workshops with clients with staggeringly consistent results. Try the test for yourself now rather than take my story as the truth:

Exercise: How to use the mind-body connection

Stand up and allow yourself to feel fed up, depressed or simply in the doldrums.

After doing so, shake the feeling off.

Now stand up straight with your shoulders back and your head looking up at the ceiling. Make sure your muscles are all relaxed and that you have a big grin across your face. While holding that position, do everything you can to feel fed up, depressed or in the doldrums.

Did you manage it?

If not, then you are amongst the thousands that I have had do this both face-to-face and virtually around the globe. Our emotions and bodies are linked, unless you have sociopathic tendencies! To be able to access 'fed up', we need our bodies to drop down, our heads to bow, or some other downward motion or slump of the body to happen.

If how we hold our bodies can have such a direct link to our emotions, and what we say to ourselves about external events can have such a physiological impact, then let's use this knowledge for the greater good. Now, I'm not suggesting that you walk around staring at the ceiling and grinning to make yourself feel more upbeat, as I imagine you will be referred for mental health support swiftly should you do so. What I am offering as a suggestion is that you use the knowledge that our mind, body and inner representations are linked to make change easy in the moment. How we re-present things that happen to us, the narrative we create around the event, is within our control. This then affects how we behave with others and ourselves. Realising that we can use our physiology to have a positive impact on our emotional state simply by lifting ourselves upwards and putting a smile on our face can have life-changing implications if owned and practised regularly.

In cases where equity has not been present in someone's inner narrative, I have noticed that what they say to themselves is a hindrance at best and the cause of the inequity at worst. Ever thought things like, 'They won't take me seriously because I'm a woman/too young/not experienced enough', or started sentences with, 'Women are…'? These inner narratives affect how we hold ourselves and change our behaviour towards others. Starting with an internal response that says 'no' in some way, or puts doubt in our minds, is a sure-fire way to stop us from fulfilling our potential. Having the courage to say 'yes', or 'I can', to ourselves first can be the difference that makes the difference.

Internal dialogue – your rackets

Our internal voices can have varied tones and come from different 'parts' of our unconscious. Within all of us, there are subpersonalities at play, and they all have a differing view and purpose. Think for a moment about the facets of yourself you show when you are with friends compared to the version of you who runs that meeting at work. Or the behaviours you demonstrate at the sports field while cheering on your child or favourite team versus those you show when caring for a sick child or elderly relative. Human beings are complex, and our experiences growing up affect our responses to situations. These are linked to the inner voice. Our internal world holds emotions, some of which are authentic feelings and some of which come from our family script and so are running automatically and often unconsciously. These family scripts can help explain why individuals and families repeat patterns of behaviour – for example, mealtimes with kids or how to discipline. In psychology, specifically the psychotherapeutic model of transactional analysis, those emotions or feelings that come from our family script are known as racket feelings.

How our caregivers responded to us when we were little sets a pattern of behaviour, or racket, that continues throughout life. Often this is happening unconsciously. For example, if you grew up in an environment where if you felt anger then it wasn't allowed or was punished, you most likely will hold in anger as an adult and won't have learned how to healthily process the feeling. It may be that you learned that when anger was felt, it was more acceptable to cry, and this got you the love or response that you needed at that time. The secondary emotion in this circumstance is the one others experience and not the actual feeling. The meaning we made of the words and actions of those adults who were around us get stored in that child state and resurface in adulthood to inform our behaviours, especially when under stress.

Exercise: Reflect on scripts

Think back to your childhood and/or think about how you parent today. Which of these negative or restrictive scripts did you hear or do you say? Notice which are more likely to be said to girls and to boys. Reframing and saying different things to children, particularly before they reach the age of seven, really matters. We need to be laying foundations that can uphold the openness that is needed when we think about creating an inclusive culture that embraces difference and allows everyone to be their best selves.

Script message (not necessarily verbal)	Meaning made
'You're different.'	DON'T BELONG
'Kids are too noisy.'	DON'T BE A CHILD
'I wish I'd never had you.'	DON'T EXIST
'Why aren't you like...'	DON'T BE YOU
'Who do you think you are?'	DON'T SUCCEED
'This is the sickly one.'	DON'T BE WELL
'Be brave.'	DON'T FEEL
'You might get hurt.'	DON'T DO IT

It is part of being human to be part of families – without them we do not survive as infants. Being part of a family means you will inevitably pick up family scripts and build an understanding of how to manage your emotions as a child. Your relationships to primary and secondary emotions are set in early life. Understanding what we are doing emotionally in our daily lives is important when it comes to being in equitable relationships or building organisations where equity is necessary.

Primary emotions are the first emotions that you feel for any given event. They are the authentic response rather than the learned behaviour. Secondary emotions are feelings you experience after the primary emotion. Secondary emotions are usually more intense emotions that push people away or protect yourself in some way. They had their place when they were needed to protect you as a child, but as adults in society we need to be able to manage our primary emotions or we will not be able to face difficult circumstances and create healthy change that can be sustained. For us to be able to embrace differences in others, we need to recognise the primary emotion that is called up and work with that. Identifying the rackets we run that hide the true root emotions can take us on a merry dance which avoids the painful truth. Only when we can dance with the pain can we make lasting shifts in our beliefs, our behaviours and our automated responses and scripts.

Exercise: Primary vs Secondary Emotions – How to tell the difference

Question	Primary	Secondary
Is your emotion a direct response to something that just happened?	❑ Yes	
After the event, did the emotion go away?	❑ Yes	
Is your emotion getting stronger with time?		❑ Yes
Is it ambiguous and hard to interpret?		❑ Yes

To break societal cycles that hold different genders in a state of what is right or wrong to show emotionally, we must first unpick and work on our own bias and patterns. When you think about the societal norms that run around gender, it isn't surprising that the rackets that are being run affect gender equity in the workplace and across society at large. These unwritten rules and expectations can control our behaviours as well as our embedded, unconscious beliefs, which can mean that we run patterns that reinforce the past.

Breaking out of the gender norm rackets that you may be running starts with knowing what they might be for you. Gender norms fit within most family scripts as they are the socially and culturally accepted principles that govern the expected behaviour of women, men, girls and boys in society.

European Institute for Gender Equality definition of gender norms

'Gender norms are ideas about how women and men should be and act. Internalised early in life, gender norms can establish a life cycle of gender socialisation and stereotyping.'

When we consider the stereotyping that has been traditionally held as truth over generations, it is easy to understand how the inequity has been upheld by both genders in many cases. These stereotypes can be damaging for all concerned, and even when I think of my own family and how my husband and I consciously make the effort to buck most of those on this list in our day-to-day lives, I still find myself in conversation with my mum, playing to the script in my family where the assumption is that Marcus needs to work as he's the breadwinner and I have more time to get family things organised.

1. Men are defenders

2. Men are leaders

3. Men are the breadwinners

4. Women are passive

5. Women are emotional

6. Women are carers

Having explored all this, the positive here is to know that our inner voices, the rackets we run and our family scripts are all ours, so we have choice and the ability to change what they say. Once we are aware of what we have running, we can do the work that is needed to make change. For some, that can be as simple as catching yourself in the moment and doing something different. For others, it may involve working with a therapist or coach to get to the root cause and make the change in a way that will stick.

As I reflect on the rackets I experience as the mum of a child with complex needs, including autism, ADHD and attachment challenges, one that is massively excluding and impactful is the judgement you experience when out in public. We have had strangers come up to us and tell our son, mid-meltdown when his executive function is offline, that he is being naughty and must listen to Mummy. When out for lunch with a friend, I had to sit on the floor with my scarf over my son's head to help cut down the sensory overwhelm that just caused him to throw the barstool across the floor while staff and customers alike were stepping over us and tutting. These are just two examples of the way people with difference are judged on a day-to-day basis. This leads to many families like ours simply not going out. We become isolated, and our children don't get to experience everyday things that seem to be a basic human right to me. To have children who cannot play in the park unless it's empty or who cannot access school because they have different needs to be able to access education is shocking. It means that a whole section of society is excluded from life, and neurotypical people don't get experiences to learn how to create environments where we can all flourish. The things that enable neurodiverse children to thrive also enable all children to grow. Whole-school strategies that are nurturing and come from a belief that every child has a right to education mean that no child is stigmatised by their additional needs, be they physical, attachment-based or a neurodivergence. (The Attachment Aware Schools Project at Stoke Virtual School with Bath University is a great example of this at work.) As a society, we are missing out on new ways of thinking and living that may well be the answer to future needs and fix current issues.

All brains are equally important

'Wow! I've never painted with a feather before, it's so much fun. You have such great ideas!'

'Ah, thanks.'

The truth is, the world needs diverse thinkers for change.

Many people have the 'children should be seen and not heard' racket running. This manifested itself most clearly for me at our local church when we lived in London. Every Sunday, I would help run the 'Messy Church' Sunday school, and at around 11am we would take all the children into the main church from the hall. We would all go and sit at the front on the floor and hear amongst the announcements which child would be taking the teddy bear home as a reward for good behaviour. Invariably this meant they had kept quiet and queued up to join the main congregation without noise. One week, my son 'won' the privilege, and as he was handed the bear, the vicar joked about how shocked he was because Nick never sits still or pays attention. He wasn't curious to find out that for Nick to even be in the space with other children was a major achievement for him due to his sensory processing challenges. It was instead deemed poor behaviour because they saw it as a choice that he was clapping and moving. Their judgement was that he was choosing to be disruptive and break the rules. Even when I attempted to help their thinking and broaden the options for them to consider that he might be doing it to regulate his sensory overwhelm, it fell on deaf ears, and the inner racket of the clergy still ran. 'Children should be seen and not heard' was their embedded belief, and the mindset was stuck.

If we are doing this with our young people in a safe and caring environment like a Sunday school, then what hope do we have of building inclusive environments for adults with difference? Morally and financially, as a society it makes sense to set up our schools, workplaces, governments and communities in a way that allows us to utilise the talents of all people. The impact on self-esteem for children with special educational needs leads to delays in learning and education at best and prison at worst. Getting this wrong matters. We must find ways to change this now, or the future generational impact will be huge and potentially devastating. The cost to society, let alone the moral obligation, is enough to push us towards creating more inclusive education, community and organisational systems. The stats below certainly demonstrate a need.

A 2021 report by the Chief Inspector of Prisons titled 'Neurodiversity in the Criminal Justice System' suggested it's entirely possible that half of the people entering the prison system can 'be expected to have some form of neurodivergent condition which impacts their ability to engage'.

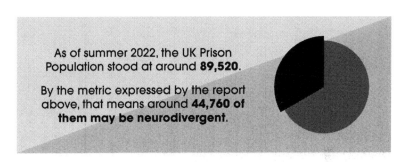

As of summer 2022, the UK Prison Population stood at around **89,520**.

By the metric expressed by the report above, that means around **44,760 of them may be neurodivergent.**

Children in prison are twice as likely to have special educational needs as those in the general population. Data from the Ministry of Justice reveals that 30 per cent of children who entered custody over 2018–19 were assessed as having special educational needs or disabilities. Separate government data shows that less than 15 per cent of children nationally fall into this category.

Tip: How to change your personal rackets

1. Notice your racket

2. Be curious about what else might be true

3. Choose to change your response

4. Practise the new response and be kind to yourself when you get it wrong

Breaking patterns and stopping autopilot

It's a very human thing to have habitual behaviours and patterns of thinking. Most of the time, these can be really useful as they save time. Who doesn't love a shortcut? Sometimes, however, these patterns lead to unintended outcomes – some minor and some more impactful. The autopilot that we run on a daily basis to do so many of our daily tasks can easily become a real hurdle to effectiveness and the very act that means we exclude anything that is different, including people. Autopilot is usually useful for the mundane day-to-day tasks, like our commute, school run or process-focused work, as it means we aren't using up energy thinking about routes or methods. Anything that impacts others needs a certain conscious thought because autopilot simply will not work.

Being on autopilot can have a detrimental impact on our own health, mood and ability to think creatively. Research has shown that by changing everyday patterns, we can up our productivity and creativity substantially. We can literally create new neural pathways in our brains by simply mixing up our usual route to a place where we frequently go. The more new pathways we can create, the greater elasticity our brain will maintain. The more plasticity our brains have, the more open we are to new thinking, new ways of working and simply noticing difference in a non-judgemental way. When we moved to London for work, I wanted to live somewhere where I could take many different routes to work. I wanted to be able to develop a more flexible mindset and be better able to keep up with my husband's neurodiverse brain (he has a million ideas a minute). This meant choosing a flat where I could walk to work in 45 minutes, taking around 15 different routes, adding in a bus journey down either Abbey Road or the Finchley Road or calling an Uber. The impact of living there and practising this daily ritual of taking a different route soon had a positive impact on my creative brain and built my ability to think more tangentially.

To change the world into a place where difference is celebrated and where the talents of every person are able to flourish requires flexibility. We need to notice patterns of chatter that our inner voices have. Are we saying things that keep us stuck on autopilot? Are we allowing others to say things that hold us in their assumptions and in past thinking? If we are, then know that we can make a change. Sometimes, simply by noticing the pattern and naming it, a shift can happen. Awareness and insight provide choice.

Changing the narrative may require more, though, and it helps to be able to build the new habit in everyday life. Allowing yourself the space to notice is the first step. Meditation is a great way to build the ability to notice more as it slows us, de-stresses us and has a positive effect on productivity. Not everyone enjoys the idea of meditating. In fact, many of us find the idea of meditating each day an anathema – it's a real turn-off, and the idea of staying still is frustrating, not relaxing! So it is great to know that building in moments of 'stilling' throughout your day can be as impactful as a more traditional meditation session. Take a moment of stilling as you load the washing machine by allowing yourself to pause and notice your breathing, bring attention to your body and get out of your mind. Or, as those traffic lights change to red, instead of getting annoyed at being slowed down, choose to embrace the gift of the few moments you have been given to take some deep breaths to fully expand your lungs and, in so doing, calm your vagus nerve.[1] These are just two examples of when you might meditate or still. Find the ones that work for you and build them into your daily life.

Exercise: PAUSE – A simple frame to regroup

This technique is perfect for those of us with busy lives. Take 30 seconds out and refocus, recharge and shift your energy from autopilot. It can be done at your desk as you trawl through the many emails you receive each day, as you reach for the next tool out of your toolbox, or as you play with your kids at the park.

P = **Pause** for a moment and interrupt your 'autopilot'.

A = **Attend** to the breath and locate the feeling of the breath in your body.

U = **Use** the out-breath to let go of any tension in the body.

S = **Sense** what is present – what are you thinking, feeling, hearing, seeing?

E = **Engage** again with your activities.

Words have the power to build or destroy

Often, when we think about difference, inclusion and equity, we focus on protected characteristics like age, disability, gender reassignment, marriage and civil partnership, pregnancy and maternity, race, religion or belief, sex, and sexual orientation. While I wholeheartedly acknowledge that it is absolutely imperative that the legal standing as laid out in the Equality Act of 2010 is upheld, it is the day-to-day happenings and their impact that I am focusing on here. Everyday language matters. Words are powerful. There are so many common phrases that hold women in a historical 'less than' place that we often don't even notice. Really prominent examples are 'career woman' or 'working mother'. Ever heard people use the phrase 'career man' or 'working father'? Didn't think so! Words are one of the ways that the patriarchy is held in place. As humans, we use on average around 16,000 words a day, and by the time we are adults (unless it is a second language) we choose them unconsciously. So we need to be kind to ourselves when we get things wrong or are using a word or expression that in 2024 seems insensitive or even archaic. Our generation, geography, culture and education lead to norming of certain words and phrases. They become second nature, with us often never having reflected on the literal meaning or how they might land with others.

Some words may not have a direct connection to gender, but if you look back over ancient, or even recent, history and consider whether they are used primarily with one sex, then you may be shocked. Think about words like feisty, bubbly, perky, frigid or hussy. Certainly, when I think about my own life over the last 30 years, I can only come up with examples of when they have been used for women. Many may consider words like feisty, bubbly or perky to be a compliment. I certainly have over the years, and I have even used some to refer to women that I've enjoyed working or spending time with. When you notice the roots of the words and when they were connected with women, though, you can see how they hold us in less esteem than our male counterparts. For example, bubbly refers to carbonated drinks or beverages like champagne, but is also used to refer to personality. It is widely thought that the use of the word to describe a woman came about in the 1920s flapper era when prohibition ruled and champagne was a much-loved drink in the clubs of the time. It was seen as frivolous, light and not something to be taken seriously (compared to a man's drink like bourbon). Women were in many ways making social strides towards equality, with shorter hair, hemlines and voting rights, and yet they were being referred to as bubbly as an endearing but clearly sexist way of diminishing their intelligence.

I find it's a good check to notice language and think, 'If I flip it to a male reference point, would I say it?' If the answer is no, then I find a different word. This isn't about being politically correct, in my view. It's about using the power of language to change the narrative. To shift cultural norms, we must shift how we talk about each other. It's everyday conversations that set the tone of what is okay.

Know your impact

If we want to get to equity in our working lives and more broadly in society, the one thing we can all do is look first to ourselves and notice the impact we have on our world and the people in it. If you are a leader, are you actively and explicitly setting up your teams and organisations to be places where all can flourish? Or are you more focused on just getting the tasks done? If you are a parent or spend time with young people, are you considering the beliefs you might be embedding for the next generation? We set norms and hold them in place through the stories we tell, the behaviours we show and the actions we take. When we are in positions of power, whether in a family, community or organisational setting, we have responsibilities and the opportunity to change things. Being mindful of what bedtime story we might read and the roles that genders are given in them is one small yet impactful thing we can do. Not playing into the idea of gendered colours for children is another. Maybe on this one you might be thinking, 'Who really cares about that?' or 'What's the big deal?' Assigning colours based on gender sends an unconscious message to children that if you are a boy, you must like blue, and you must not like pink as it's not manly. Or if, like me, you like blue and not pink, then you are considered a 'tomboy', which doesn't mean you are a strong female but that you do not know how to be a 'proper' girl. These labels and assumptions that are laid upon us at a young age then play out in what we believe to be possible for us as adults as we grow. We begin to live up to the stereotypes. So if we want less stereotypes, less sexism and less prejudice, then a good place to start might be in breaking some. Let's go for a rainbow of colour instead.

In a work setting when we are a leader or manager of others, we must raise our own awareness of our impact. Every word that comes out of a boss's mouth is taken as fact by most people. Each action sets a tone for what is acceptable behaviour around here. When I am coaching leaders in organisations, a common topic we explore is around language and impact. It can be a shock for some that they are perceived in a particular way by those who work for them. One example that comes to mind is when a female leader named Julie, who I was coaching as part of a talent programme, came to talk to me about a problem she was having with their IT director. Julie was highly skilled and hugely qualified, she had years of experience in her area of expertise, and she was seen as a director of the future by the organisation. This didn't help one jot, though, when her IT director referred to her as a donkey in a team meeting. Through conversation with him, I discovered that it had happened at a point when there was some 'banter' and the team, in which she was the only female, were calling each other after animals as a joke. The director was the most senior person in the room and chairing the meeting, but in the joking he had forgotten himself and joined in. He hadn't considered how the very chair he sat in gave his words more power. The impact of his words had sent Julie into an internal conversation with herself about the 'why' – 'Why did he say that? Does he think I'm stupid?' It had got to a point where she was considering leaving the organisation. Her reputation mattered to her. When she raised her concerns about what had happened and the impact it had on her, the director initially reacted in a way that labelled Julie as a drama queen and overly sensitive. He was one step away from literally telling her to 'grow a pair' and 'man up'! When challenged to consider if he would think these things and use those descriptions if a male member of the team had the same concerns, he realised that he had some stereotypes running. He also realised that it was his responsibility to ensure that permissions and limitations were noticed and upheld in meeting environments. With positional power, you have the opportunity to create inclusive environments every day and, in doing so, get the best from your team. You create a space where people feel safe enough to offer opinions and thoughts, to bring all of themselves. Being part of the 'banter' just isn't good enough.

Prefaces and disclaimers

How we begin interactions with others has a bigger impact than most people realise. The words we use literally tell others' brains what to filter in and what to filter out while they listen to whatever we are sharing. When creating an environment where there is equality of voice and equity is present, we need to own what we say and step into our own light. Dumbing things down or overusing modesty will not help with creating credibility or enable you to be fully understood. Think back for a moment – have you ever started a conversation or presentation by saying something like, 'This might be silly, but…' or 'It's just a thought, but…'? If you have, then chances are that you are giving away your power and gravitas. Planting the seed that what you are about to say could be silly tells the listener's brain to filter what you say for things that are silly. Every second, there are two million bits of data coming at you, and the neurotypical brain filters so that we don't become overwhelmed. This filtering is necessary and unconscious. Without it, the brain would not be able to process what is coming in and make sense of it. One way this filtering happens is by noticing the flags that the person communicating with you gives. If I asked you to look around the environment you are currently in as you read this book and count how many things there are that are blue, you would do that easily. If I then get you to close your eyes and tell me how many red things there are, you most likely will struggle. This is because I had flagged blue as the priority in my opening sentence. Try it out and see for yourself.

In Deborah Tannen's research for her book *Talking from 9 to 5*, she discovered that when it comes to communicating in the workplace, the employees who get heard tend to speak directly, loudly and at greater length than their co-workers. Being too polite backfires. Many people try to avoid seeming presumptuous by prefacing their statements with a disclaimer such as, 'I don't know if this will work' or 'You've probably already thought of this'. Such disclaimers only cause the rest of the communication to be ignored or diminished. Making sure the preface we use directs our audience's brain to filter in the way that we want sets us up for success.

Now I know that simply telling you to speak up and stop using prefaces or you telling people in your team to speak up doesn't work! Some people simply need time to reflect before speaking. Others, often women, have embedded behaviours that stem from being taught to be polite and a 'good girl' when growing up. So the idea of stating an opinion outright seems rude! To be able to fulfil our potential and have the impact that we want in the world, whether it's at work or more broadly in the community, we need to reframe speaking up. Making sure that in any group environment there is equality of turn-taking and equity of voice is the way to attain high performance. Instead of running your 'good girl' messaging, tell yourself that you are an ambassador and you are bringing forward the voice for your tribe. By sharing your opinion, you will start to write a different narrative for the girls and young women who will follow. Set a different tone. Speak up and speak out. We can be polite and softly spoken or roaring from the rafters – all that matters is that your voice comes forth.

Companies that want to take advantage of contributions from all employees need to have managers who foster environments that allow for different preferences and needs. To allow those who are more reflective to contribute, make sure you either set them up with what topics and questions are to be explored at the meeting at least 48 hours before or split the meeting into two time slots with a gap between them so that people can go away, consider their opinions and come back ready to share in part two.

You could also use an adapted version of the Japanese technique of *nemawashi*. This is where the facilitator meets with the participants one-to-one before the meeting. The facilitator can then make a presentation that includes a variety of opinions and saves face for those whose suggestions aren't followed. Where meeting is too onerous, sending a 'pre-meeting questionnaire' can work as well. Ultimately, flexing to not only accommodate but also be generative will lead to better results for individuals, teams, organisations and the world.

Story

I was working with a female leader in banking named Jo, and we were setting coaching objectives in the initial contracting meeting with her boss. The driver for the coaching provision was that Jo was seen as having great potential, and her appraisals for the last few years had been exceptional, but she had gone for promotion to a regional director role twice and had fallen at the last interview. Feedback was always that the interview panel all believed that she had what it took technically to do the role but that they didn't have the confidence in her ability to be assertive or handle difficult situations when they arose. Her boss, Richard, shared that they needed to see her demonstrate greater gravitas day-to-day. A key reason for having these tripartite meetings when setting up coaching in organisations is to enable me to dig underneath the presenting objective and to truly understand the root. Often, there are stereotypes and assumptions at play, so if you do not catch them at the beginning, you can find yourself working with the wrong person or with a missing ingredient. Upon exploring the story from both Jo's and Richard's perspectives, it became clear that they were both making judgements based on unconscious patterns and rackets. Jo was triggering the pattern by using certain words and behaving in a particular way.

On the three days that they worked in the office together, whenever Jo had something to ask or run by Richard, she would head over to his room. She'd tap on the already open door and wait in the doorway for him to say it was okay to come in, then ask, 'Have you got some time?' For her, this was polite, but for him it showed a lack of confidence. The men who had previously received the promotions in the team would see the door open, walk in, and say, 'I need ten minutes with you. Now okay? Or shall I come back later?' They correctly assumed that they had the right to his time and that his door being open meant he was approachable. It wasn't that what Jo was doing was wrong at all. It simply sent a signal to Richard that she unconsciously wasn't worth his time or that what she had to say wasn't important. The work we went on to do during the coaching led to Jo connecting with her own positional power, keeping her authentic gentle nature AND owning her space to speak up.

Triggers

All humans have triggers – some that are really useful and others that may cause an unintended negative consequence. In this context, it may be useful to clarify what I mean when I say trigger. What I am referencing as a trigger is a person, place, thing or situation that elicits an intense or unexpected emotional response. Any sensory stimulus can be a potential trigger, from a person's tone of voice to a smell. Triggers are unique and differ from threats. Essentially, it is when a non-threatening stimulus is triggering an automatic, reptilian brain, fight-or-flight response, a response that is bigger than what is actually needed in the moment. When you think about this, it is a core thing to be able to understand, accept and begin to build strategies for managing if you want to build a more inclusive society. Without raising your awareness of what your own triggers may be or considering things that you may be doing that unwittingly trigger others, it is likely that, at best, you are using a lot of energy to regulate yourself or, in a small but frequent way, damaging your relationships with others. Each time the stress response of fight-or-flight kicks in, it sets off a chain of reactions that result in an increased heart rate, blood pressure and breathing rate. Our bodies can stay in fight-or-flight for 20–60 minutes after the perceived threat has gone, which is how long it takes for the parasympathetic nervous system to return to its pre-arousal levels. The energy we can save by avoiding the trigger (or reprogramming it if it's our own) is huge!

During the pandemic, glimpses of progress were made in the supermarkets when they started to introduce a set hour during the week that was autism-friendly – times when the lighting was less harsh and the music was off or turned down. Anything that can reduce the sensory input for those with sensory processing difficulty makes places and activities more accessible. Fewer triggers means more capacity to manage in the environment. For those who work in open-plan office environments, just imagine how excluding that can be for our neurodiverse friends and colleagues. How much energy must they have to use simply to manage to be present in their surroundings? And how many choose not to work in certain roles because it would simply be untenable? The environments we create have the ability to exclude without us even realising, and solutions can often be easily found. Asking and researching options can lead to solutions that are good for all – not just those who have the need.

Amongst looked-after children, **82% were identified with special educational needs**, compared to 34% of those who had not been in care.

Just **7.2%** of looked-after children achieved the grade 5 'good pass' threshold in GCSE English and mathematics compared to 40.1% of non-looked-after children.

A wonderful example that is currently being used in many Ukrainian schools is that they have changed the traditional harsh-sounding end-of-class/break bell to a gentler, more musical sound. With the war, the shocking noise of bombs and sirens has become all too familiar to the children, and so as to not trigger the inevitable trauma response that a harsh, loud sound might make, they have changed it. Hopefully, here in the UK, our children will never know war in the way that so many around the world do, and yet there are many children in our education system who have trauma responses that are coded from other traumatic life experiences. As the mother of our wonderful adopted son, I have had the privilege of learning and living through how standard mainstream school activities and ways of teaching can trigger so many 'looked after' children.[2]

For us, the reality of the impact of schools not understanding trigger responses was when our five-year-old was put at risk of permanent exclusion. Even though we were working with the special educational needs coordinator to organise diagnosis and assessment for additional needs (we didn't know about his autism and ADHD at this point), they kept putting him in situations where he could not manage. They punished him when he 'failed' and allowed him to be called a naughty boy. Children live up to the labels they are given. A room with 20+ four- to five-year-olds is going to be loud and have an overwhelming amount of sensory input. If they all go out to break through one small door, they will be touching and bumping into each other. These were all triggers for our little boy and often led to him losing the ability to speak. Without words, he would communicate in the only way available, which was to hit out to stop others from coming near. Many times, the classroom had to be evacuated during a meltdown to keep everyone safe. The system failed by continuing to put a child who quite clearly couldn't manage the environment repeatedly back into it, expecting a different outcome. Small changes could have led to very different outcomes, but the mentality of cause-and-effect thinking, coupled with an 'everyone must be treated the same' attitude, meant that those who have different needs were excluded. Punishment was never going to teach in this circumstance. It wasn't a rational choice – it was a survival instinct. As adults, we need to take responsibility for finding inclusive solutions. You wouldn't punish a child for not being able to walk up steps if they need a wheelchair or force a child with a nut allergy to have Nutella for lunch. So what makes it okay to punish children (and adults) who have hidden disabilities that mean they cannot fit the socially acceptable norm? Finding a more creative way that works for all will lead to the next generation growing up with a more inclusive mindset.

So, as a parent of a child who has additional needs that you are fighting the system to get support for, you can get a feel for the impact that the harsh language and instructions have when you are told that your child is excluded and therefore unable to go to school. On the next page, you'll find an extract from the exclusion letter you receive whether your child is five (like ours was at the time) or 15, irrespective of any disability or extenuating circumstances.

We can never know a person's trigger or needs in terms of environment, so it's good practice to be mindful of possible stimuli that could set off unintended consequences.

Remember that some triggers have been embedded due to specific lived experiences. For example, if you grew up in a household where there was a lot of arguing or domestic abuse, then it is likely that you will have a greater sensitivity or hypervigilance when there is a raised voice. Or it may be that when walking into a certain type of atmosphere, it takes you back to those times when you were unsafe. These can send you into a fight, flight or freeze (or flop for some people) response. This is true for many of us, even if, rationally, we know that the current situation is not a physical threat.

Dear (Parent's Name)

I am writing to inform you of my decision to suspend (Child's Name) for (specify period). This means that (he/she) will not be allowed in school for this period. The suspension (begins/began) on (date) and ends on (date). I realise that this suspension may well be upsetting for (Child's Name), you and your family, but the decision to suspend (Child's Name) has not been taken lightly.

(Child's Name) has been suspended for this fixed period because (reasons for the suspension — as a *minimum* should include a summary of the incident and behaviour which led to taking the decision to suspend the pupil).

Since your child is of compulsory school age, you have a duty to ensure that your child is not present in a public place during school hours for the duration of this suspension (specify dates) unless there is reasonable justification for this. I must inform you that you may he prosecuted or receive a fixed penalty notice from the local authority if your child is present in a public place during school hours or the specified dates. It will be for you to show that there is reasonable justification.

Triggers affect people differently so can elicit positive or negative responses, and it's important to remember that not all significant events cause triggers. Here are some examples of triggers which I think bring this to life:

Auditory triggers

When he was five years old, Michael found himself face to face with his neighbours' German Shepherd dogs. They were growling and showing their teeth. His mum came and very quickly picked him up to safety, so nothing happened, but whenever he now hears a growl, his body freezes. This has caused many arguments in his marriage because, having grown up in a household with three Labradors, his wife, Jo, finds the sound of dogs play-fighting really comforting, so doesn't recognise the trigger or empathise with Michael.

Visual triggers

Having grown up in West Cornwall, I had many experiences of nearly being run over on country roads when out walking, or later, when I passed my driving test, of being made to reverse a long way to find a passing place. My consistent memory was that the cause of these experiences were older men in flat caps driving 'sensible' vehicles (most local farm folks near me fit this description). So whenever I see a man driving with a flat cap, even if it's in a city, I take evasive action well before anything actually happens, and I find that my heart is racing.

Kinaesthetic triggers

The feeling of scratchy net sides on a travel cot for our little boy when he was a baby meant comfort and safety to him. In his foster parents' home, that is where he slept next to their bed. We didn't know this when he came to us, so we settled him into his wooden cot, and only when he got distressed during the night did we, through conversation with his foster mum, realise that he had been triggered by the change and needed the exact same material to feel safe in his new environment.

Olfactory triggers

Arguably the most powerful sense for triggers, smell is thought to be the most connected to evoking memories. For me, the smell of Old Spice aftershave can take me right back to my childhood home and playing Lego with my dad. It's as if I am there with him today, even though it was 40 years ago. That is a really pleasant memory for me, but I know for a friend that the same smell compels her to run away, as it was worn by someone who attacked her when she was walking home from school as a ten-year-old.

Gustatory triggers

As a teenager, Maggie grew up in a house where there was domestic abuse. Every Friday, her family would have a fish-and-chip supper, and during the meal her father would come home, having gone to the pub after work, and pick a fight (physical and emotional) with her mother. The taste of fish or chips from a takeaway is now something that makes her muscles tighten and her stomach turn to a point of nausea.

To get the most from people and enable us to live to our full potential, we need to consider our impact on those around us. For those who are being impacted, there is often a choice we can make that will enable us to operate in difficult circumstances. However, for the world (society and organisations) to truly get our best, we need to make changes that allow people's energy to be used for creating rather than coping. A personal example that comes to mind for me is when I think back to my twenties and early thirties when I would actively, although unconsciously, defeminise myself in the workplace. I had made an unconscious connection between being female and being held back or put down. Growing up in the 1970s and 80s meant that whether I looked to the norms in my small home town of Camborne in Cornwall or to the media, it was clear that women were 'less than' in some way. It was the men who were the breadwinners and who held the power. Your biggest dream outside of the home would be to become a Charlie's Angel, one of Benny Hill's dancers or a beauty queen! To stand out as a girl or woman in ways that weren't to do with how you looked meant you would be put down, hurt, labelled in a derogatory way or told you were too dominant. It took years for me to work through the repeated feedback in the workplace that I was too opinionated and too dominant in conversations and that I needed to be more modest and thoughtful. The comments were from well-meaning mentors and bosses, so I took them on. It was years before I realised that my male colleagues who had similar traits and behaviours to me were being praised for being assertive, taking charge and being decisive, and they were being encouraged to share their successes in order to build their profiles and gain promotion. Not quite the same as being modest! The term 'ladylike' was no longer acceptable as it was seen quite rightly as being discriminatory, but the feedback was most definitely through the lens of how a lady should be.

Exercise: Communicating triggers

If you've experienced trauma and have triggers, the debate surrounding triggers and the use of trigger warnings can be uncomfortable.

Maybe you've experienced pushback when trying to tell someone you're feeling triggered. Or maybe you're self-conscious about telling someone about your triggers because they tend to have a knee-jerk reaction to any mention of the topic.

If someone often brings up triggering topics to you, these tips can help you broach the subject in a productive way:

- **State your feelings as specifically as possible.** 'When you said X, it made me feel anxious and afraid because of my history.'

- **State a boundary.** 'It's hard for me to talk about X. If it comes up in conversation, I'll need to leave the room.'

- **Ask for a warning.** 'I know it's hard to avoid the subject of X. Could you let me know beforehand if it's going to come up?'

As you navigate these conversations, remember that trauma is a complex but very real experience that affects people in a variety of ways. Be open to adapting, listening and pacing your own and their needs.

Equality is not the same as equity

In many conversations or articles I read, I notice that the words equity and equality are used interchangeably. They have a very different day-to-day felt impact, though, so I believe it is important for us to be clear about what we are aiming for here. Knowing your goals and focus enables you to hone your behaviours and make sure your language and actions are aligned with true equity.

Defining equity and equality – so what's the difference?

Although equality is a good thing in many instances, it is simply not enough to make the change that is truly needed across society and organisational life to make a real difference. If we want a world (or organisation, community, school… insert your part of this here) where all people can fulfil their potential regardless of gender, race, sexuality or other difference, then we need to be striving for more. Equality is making sure that everyone is treated the same. For many, I can imagine you are now nodding your head in agreement, saying something like, 'Well of course, that's what is fair.' If you are thinking that, then you are correct. It is important that each person or group is given the same access to information and resources. What we need to be crystal clear on, though, is that equality alone is not enough. The difference with equity is that it is focused on the outcome rather than the input.

Equity recognises that each person has different circumstances and allocates the exact resources and opportunities needed to reach an equal outcome.

A good example of equality is the recent support given to households because of the fuel crisis. Government subsidies were available to all people, whether they were rich or poor. This is not equitable, and yet we are all treated equally. Fairness here would require people to be treated based on financial need and not on whether they use fuel. Examples of equity lie in things like decisions by companies to consciously look for a female director for their board that is composed of all men. Or with affirmative action policies or those often referred to as quotas, things that are for certain marginalised sections of society, like Disability Living Allowance (DLA). The irony in our current society is that even where the policy is in place to enable equity, such as the DLA, I cannot begin to describe how difficult the system makes it for those in need of these allowances to receive them. The DLA application is around 72 pages long, and you have to complete it annually. If you are in need of DLA, it is likely you are already in a situation of high stress, and many may require it due to a learning disability, age-related long-term disability, or challenge such as autism/ADHD, which makes completing this type of application impossible without support. This could be another chapter in a different book, but I do believe it is worth noting that those of us who can influence the system must look at how processes impact access.

Let's look at an example to bring this difference between equality and equity to life in an everyday scenario. Imagine you are at a sports event where they have put a safety barrier up that is two metres high. If you are 1.8m in height, you will need a box of 0.5m to comfortably see over and have a great time watching the match. If you are 1.6m tall or 1.2m tall, having the same box of 0.5m is equal in terms of the resource given but does not solve the problem (equality). Equity would be that the 1.8m person gets a box of 0.5m, the 1.6m person gets a 0.7m box, and the 1.2m person a 1.1m box. This would mean that all could comfortably see over and watch the match. As a systemic coach, though, I am driven to go one step further and look at the root cause of the issue. The two-metre barrier has a practical and important purpose in terms of crowd safety, so we cannot simply knock it down, but it blocks the view for many in the front rows. To systemically solve the problem, you could replace the barrier with a clear safety Perspex wall or toughened metal cage fencing that you can see through. This would mean that whatever your size, you can see the match. For me, this tale highlights that it's the way of thinking when problem-solving or creating environments and cultures that needs to shift. Being more outcome-focused and considering different needs can only lead to a better situation for all.

Common misunderstandings

In organisational settings when conversations begin about diversity, equity and inclusion, I often hear comments about how unfair it is to prioritise specific groups. Sometimes this is about women, and other times it's about race. Whatever the group being referenced is, there is a growing sense of marginalisation being felt by those who currently are in the majority and have privilege – white men. Oftentimes, there are approaches to creating equity in the workplace that are excluding for those who have been in positions of privilege for some time. This cannot be the answer as it continues the same dynamic that is the current problem. It makes one group more important and, in doing so, sets them up as the new perpetrator, while the other then has to become the victim. This means that, inevitably, a rescuer is hooked in. This drama triangle means we will be stuck in the repetitive pattern of behaviour that the patriarchal nature of organisations/society has at this present moment.

The Karpman Drama Triangle

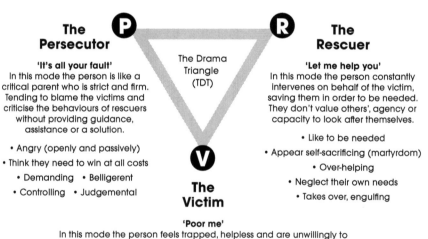

The Persecutor (P)

'It's all your fault'
In this mode the person is like a critical parent who is strict and firm. Tending to blame the victims and criticise the behaviours of rescuers without providing guidance, assistance or a solution.

- Angry (openly and passively)
- Think they need to win at all costs
- Demanding • Belligerent
- Controlling • Judgemental

The Drama Triangle (TDT)

The Rescuer (R)

'Let me help you'
In this mode the person constantly intervenes on behalf of the victim, saving them in order to be needed. They don't value others', agency or capacity to look after themselves.

- Like to be needed
- Appear self-sacrificing (martyrdom)
- Over-helping
- Neglect their own needs
- Takes over, engulfing

The Victim (V)

'Poor me'
In this mode the person feels trapped, helpless and are unwillingly to take responsibility for their undesirable circumstances. They don't value themselves or feel they have the power to change their lives.

- Blaming of persecutors • Whinging and complaining
- Manipulative • Anxious and fretful
- Seeking for Rescuer to solve the problem for them

Many trainings on the topic of diversity, equity and inclusion have an inbuilt focus on teaching us how to 'walk a mile' in marginalised groups' shoes, to help us understand what things are like for them and to then be able to change our approach so as not to offend or exclude. With this focus, it sets up a disempowered dynamic as it often creates fear in those who are attempting to make things better – fear of getting it wrong! On hearing trainers saying things like, 'You have to be very careful what you say, or you might offend people,' I have witnessed the wide-eyed response of participants first-hand. I'm pretty sure this left them feeling less equipped to interact with those they perceived as different from before the training. This type of instruction will not make the world a more inclusive place and in fact may actually lead to the opposite. It most likely will create greater polarisation as people have their insecurities triggered. It will hook anyone with a fear of failure, a need to be 'perfect' and get things right, as well as those who worry about hurting others. It will also repel those who have a 'Don't you tell me what to do' button. They most likely will jump on the side of believing this is positive discrimination and a bad thing. This is where I find it useful to look at things through the lens of the Drama Triangle. It is a model of human behaviour developed by Stephen Karpman that is most commonly used in psychotherapeutic settings to help people understand the roles they take in conflict situations. It is also commonly used in organisational settings for similar purposes. Once you can understand which role you tend to identify with, then you can make a change. The triangle is a co-dependent dynamic where each point is reliant on the others existing to maintain itself. It's important here to note that when we say 'victim', it does not refer to an actual victim but to someone who may take a 'poor me' stance and see themselves as being at the receiving end of others' bad behaviour. In the dynamic of the drama triangle, if the victim were effectively helped, then there would be no need for a rescuer. In the same way, the victim cannot claim to be victimised unless they can point the finger at a persecutor. These roles feel comfortable and familiar to most of us as we will have had experiences throughout our earlier lives that showed us how to 'do' them. This comfort means it often feels safe, even when the reality is damaging. The drama triangle will keep playing out in our lives as it is an innate part of being human. Those who feel at home in one of the roles will seek out or attract others into the other roles to fulfil the 'game'. The tragedy here is that the dynamics of the triangle tend to spiral and so pull more people into conflict. Typically, the victim and the rescuer can justify their positions by, ironically, playing persecutor to the perceived persecutor, which shifts the original persecutor into a victim role. The original victim then becomes the rescuer, and so on. The switching of roles means that there is a generative nature to the behaviour. It takes a conscious awareness of the game, the role we have been hooked into and the courage to break the pattern for this to stop. To make lasting change in a systemic way, we need to build understanding and gain conscious awareness of the parts we play in the problem. We also need to develop a deeper courage to lean in, even if we may get it 'wrong'. The key is to come from a place of curiosity and courage and to have real conversations. Relying on rescuers to champion marginalised groups and condemn persecutors is counterproductive. It holds the triangle in place. Stepping into an empowerment dynamic, such as the one created by David Emerald, is one way to shift thinking and behaviour. See the image opposite to understand the switch in this approach.

In this approach, anyone can shift from the drama mode to the empowerment role. If you are typically drawn to getting onto your white stallion and rescuing, then instead try coaching. If you're more likely to find yourself persecuting (finding flaws and criticising or blaming), then how about constructively challenging? The most important shift here is that the victim steps into a creator role. Even if they still see themselves as a victim (poor me), then it is open to the rescuers and persecutors to refuse to continue the game. They can end the co-dependency by asking a great question and/or offering a positive challenge. By doing this, we take an active role in creating the world we want to see − one that embraces difference and includes all.

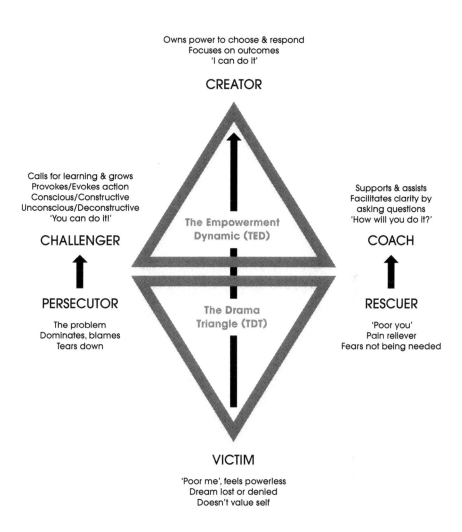

Owns power to choose & respond
Focuses on outcomes
'I can do it'

CREATOR

Calls for learning & grows
Provokes/Evokes action
Conscious/Constructive
Unconscious/Deconstructive
'You can do it!'

CHALLENGER

The Empowerment
Dynamic (TED)

Supports & assists
Facilitates clarity by
asking questions
'How will you do it?'

COACH

PERSECUTOR

The problem
Dominates, blames
Tears down

The Drama
Triangle (TDT)

RESCUER

'Poor you'
Pain reliever
Fears not being needed

VICTIM

'Poor me', feels powerless
Dream lost or denied
Doesn't value self

The feelings and the numbers

As with all things in life, there are statistics and data that tell a story, and there's how we feel about or perceive things. When I think about and step into my experiences of equality and equity, I notice that an internal tension often arises. My rational brain can tell me all it likes about how the facts are fair, but if equity doesn't exist then there is a really visceral sense of incongruence within me. Things just aren't right, and I can feel it even when I can't explain it. This incongruent feeling can occur frequently for neurodiverse families like ours. Family and friends can be well intended, and yet old scripts of what is socially acceptable or fair run unconsciously. A great example of when an intention to be inclusive is followed up by positive action was with some friends of ours who are the best 'event' throwers I've ever known. If you are invited to one of their parties, then the answer has to be yes because they are wonderful. Each summer, they have a garden festival where around 10–12 families come and camp on their land. We always get an invitation so we are treated equally, and the friend even offers us a glamping pod slightly away from where the campers will be as they understand that our son may need space to regulate. This provides the sense of equity as it makes the event accessible for us. Even with this equity, we choose to only do a day trip as the fear of a major dysregulation when in the company of many who won't get it in the same way as our friends feels too risky. So the facts and stats are all set, but the feelings are the final decision-making element. In many other instances, we are, often unintentionally or through conscious kindness, excluded from activities. Many children with a neurodiversity don't ever get invited to birthday parties for other kids in their class. When I've had conversations with other parents to understand the 'why', I discovered that for some it comes from a place of fear of not knowing what might happen, while others assume that due to his autism he wouldn't want to come or that he wouldn't even notice he was the only one not invited. Children do notice, and it has a deep effect on their self-esteem. This happens in organisations I work with as much as the family setting. As neurotypical people, we can often be fearful of things that are different from us. We need the courage to be able to sit with the discomfort and engage anyway. Ask that question. Stop your assumptions about what neurodiverse people need or feel like. Check in and include them in the discussions. If you get it wrong, that is okay as long as you repair it afterwards. This repair may take the form of an apology, and you will certainly need to own the impact without excuse. Saying 'Sorry but…' just doesn't cut it. Apologise AND resist the urge to justify your actions.

Vernā Myers, a well-known American diversity and inclusion expert and activist, puts it well with her famous quote: 'Diversity is being invited to the party; inclusion is being asked to dance.' The words in common parlance are often used interchangeably, but they are truly and strongly juxtaposed. Diversity is a fact, and inclusion is a choice. This quote goes some way to helping us make sense of the difference, although it doesn't fully capture the complexity. I would go so far as to say the aim in organisational and societal terms is for an environment where anyone who wants to get up and dance can. They don't need to wait for the person with relational or literal power to ask them.

Why it matters to include neurodiverse people

Autistic people make up approximately 1% of the population but 11% of suicides, and with estimations that there are over half a million undiagnosed autistic adults in the UK, this percentage may be higher.

- Autistic adults with no learning disability are nine times more likely to die by suicide than the general population.

- It is the second leading cause of death for autistic people. The average life expectancy for autistic people is 54.

- Up to 66% of autistic adults have considered suicide.

- Autistic children are 28 times more likely to attempt suicide.

- One study showed that 15% of autistic children had suicidal thoughts compared to 0.5% of typically developing children.

- In the 86 days leading up to the first lockdown and up to 56 days after, a quarter of young people who died by suicide were autistic or had ADHD.

See it, say it, stop it

To be able to see it, say it and then stop it, we need to hone our sensory acuity so we notice what is really going on. Without this, we can't step up and say it, let alone stop it. Once we have noticed what is happening or what we are doing that is excluding or failing to create equity, we need the courage to be able to speak up. Whether it's stopping ourselves or others, we must create connection before correction to make change possible and avoid the natural defensive reaction that all humans have to being made wrong. By building rapport and being in a relationship rather than at odds with someone, you connect, and then when you offer the correction or feedback, they are more likely to be able to hear what you have to say. Being open to hearing criticism or about something that is wrong requires there to be psychological safety. If someone doesn't feel safe, they will defend themselves and, therefore, their position. From this place, no change will ever happen.

Sensory acuity – noticing what's really going on

Our senses are multifaceted, and each of us will most likely have a bias. Mine is for the visual, so I can notice things being 'off' from a great distance – in fact, way before I can hear or feel anything, my eyes have done their work. My least preferred sense, and one I have had to work on over the years, is the auditory. Hearing things and being able to take them in fully has been a struggle. It's a muscle that practice has built in terms of skill as a coach, although for me, in times of stress or deep relaxation, it is still the first to switch off. The third main sense to keep in mind when thinking about how you might be more attuned to inequity is the felt or kinaesthetic sense. What is your embodied sense of reality in any given moment? Our gut can tell us a lot and be much quicker than our brain's executive function when attempting to work things out.

Exercise: Ways to build up your sensory acuity

1. Go to the ocean and sit down comfortably with your eyes closed. Notice what you can hear. What are the subtle sounds? Do the waves crashing closer to you sound different from those that are further away? Are there any bird sounds or noises from nature nearby? If there are birds, how many can you hear? Different species?

2. Head to a busy, more populated area like a park or town centre. Sitting still, how many different sounds can you differentiate? What are the volumes, the tones, the speed? What can you make out in the distance? What are the sensations you experience? Is there a breeze? What temperature are different parts of your body in this environment? Can you sense other people moving around near you? If so, how?

3. Over the next week when you step outside of your home, notice what you see first, what you hear first and how it feels. Write these responses in a journal, and each morning capture the same information. Then do the same thing later in the day. Are there any differences? What's missing that you would expect to see/hear/feel? Which sense did you notice first each time?

Once you have built strength in your sensory acuity, you will also need to check your generalisations and assumptions. Neurotypical brains have a super-effective filtration system that enables us to go about our daily lives without hitting sensory overwhelm. Of the two million bits of data per second that come at us, these filters only allow 134 to reach their target. So, for instance, until I mention it, you probably weren't thinking about where you are breathing from or how your left leg feels against the surface you are sitting or standing on. This is because these data points weren't relevant up until I mentioned them. It is important to know what filters you have set up as they develop throughout life based on our experiences. Left unchecked, they remain, setting us up to run old patterns that may have been useful at one point in our lives but may, at best, now be outdated. At worst, they may be having the unintended impact of creating inequalities and inequity, and stopping you from building diversity in your world. Who or what are you filtering out that your life may be all the richer for if you included them/it?

Let's explore in a bit more depth how the typical brain does this. The three main filters we run are generalisations, distortions and deletions. They are hugely useful and can also be limiting. So, for instance, you probably would want to leave in place the generalisations you make about how doors work. Imagine how exhausting it would be to walk up to every door and have to figure out how to open it! You may, though, want to update generalisations you have about who in society might want to work part-time. Spoiler alert… it's not only new mothers. It could be fathers or people who want to train to sail around the world or to go back to university and study while working. With our ageing population, it's likely that many working people need flexibility to care for older family members as well. Time is an asset that many want to balance the use of consciously in their lives, so recruiting in traditional ways for full-time or even part-time roles without thinking about how to be flexible will not get you the best talent or outcomes.

Here are some examples of how you might spot when you or others might have one of these filters running and questions you might ask to help clarify and be curious:

Deletions (of specific information)

You'll hear or say statements like: 'They always say…'

To uncover the deleted information, ask questions like: 'Who specifically…?'

Distortions (common beliefs and assumptions, value judgements, cause and effect)

Statements like: 'I can't X because Y will happen.'

Ask questions like: 'How would X'ing make Y happen?'

Generalisations (must, should, always, every, X means Y)

Statements like: 'I should do better…'

Ask questions like: 'Should according to whom?'

When we uncover and become conscious of the filters that our brains are naturally using, we open up greater choice. With greater choice, there is more possibility and you become more focused on the outcomes rather than the inputs being made by yourself and others. If we are more able to open our minds to considering that there are many different ways to get to an outcome, then we will naturally become more inclusive. It will also allow us the chance to develop greater decision-making skills as we include things that may previously have been filtered out. Contexts and needs change, so coming at any decision while automatically filtering data is likely to be flawed and limiting. By exploring what is being deleted, distorted and generalised, we uncover more of the 'truths'. The better the data, the better the decision.

The empathy lens

To be able to see it, say it and stop it effectively, we need to be confident and kind. This way, we can create change. In times of change, it is especially important to be able to access the full spectrum of emotion and properly differentiate between feelings. So when thinking about the empathy lens, we need to begin by stating that empathy differs from sympathy in quite a significant way. If we think about them as the same then we fall into a dangerous trap – when it comes to what is effective in creating change, we need more than the ability to sympathise and understand someone else's suffering. Sympathy has its place in terms of support, but to fully motivate ourselves to understand and make change, we need to be ready to truly empathise. When we empathise, in our mind's eye we are allowing ourselves to 'step into the other person's shoes', and by internally referencing our own lived experiences we are then able to connect with how it might be for them. Empathy is the ability to share someone else's feelings or experiences by imagining what it could be like to be in that person's situation. To be able to sense others' emotions and see things from their point of view is key if we want to be advocates or change agents. Empathy can help establish norms that promote inclusion and create more equitable environments. A recent example I had of where sympathy, not empathy, was behind action was at a college where I am studying elements of psychotherapy to build into my coaching practice. I had looked at the accessibility aspects before signing up and was initially delighted when, at check-in, the tutor asked about how I would like to be known over the weekend. They were interested not just in whether it was my first name or a title but also my pronoun. Once I had shared my preference for she/her and Sarah, I then went off to use the loo. It was at this point it struck me. They had taken the time and effort to make sure that the tutor was creating an inclusive environment, but when it came to the physical one, they were lacking. They had taken a good approach as far as making sure there was sloped access and an accessible toilet cubicle in the building, but they had not actually noticed that it wasn't usable! It had the requisite size door frame and the appropriate wall supports next to the toilet to help people manoeuvre out of their wheelchairs. I can imagine the project manager ticking the boxes on the check sheet to make sure they were doing what was needed during the fitting. The college team had certainly sympathised with the needs of those who were not able-bodied and wanted to make their courses open to all. What they hadn't done, though, was actually put themselves into the position of someone in a wheelchair and empathise fully. If they had, they would have noticed that to get to the toilet cubicle door that was wide enough for a chair, you had to go through a standard-sized door that a wheelchair cannot get through.

They would also have noted that once inside the cubicle, the space was not big enough to turn a chair around, so you could not use the handles to get onto the loo if you shut the door!

A key to change is to speak up when you notice something that is not okay. So, first, notice through an empathy lens and then speak up. Often, people are speaking or acting on autopilot, so it is a kindness to hold up the mirror. We don't need to be a vigilante about it and shout and scream. With the empathy lens, you will stay in a space of relationship. Remember, connection before correction is key. As we've explored before, making others wrong will only create defence and not change. Heels get dug in further, and recalcitrant behaviour ensues whenever we feel wronged. It's a survival instinct in many ways. We are wired to survive, and as such when pushed into an 'I'm right and you're wrong' conversation, it will not create the difference in behaviour that is required. Be kind and clear.

Exercise: The empathy mapping tool

To begin to build your empathy 'muscle', you need to consciously practise stepping out of your comfort zone and into others' maps of the world. This tool will enable you to practise in many different situations at home or at work. Consider using it if:

- you want to influence your child's teacher

- you need to have a developmental feedback conversation with a team member

- you work in a role that deals with customers

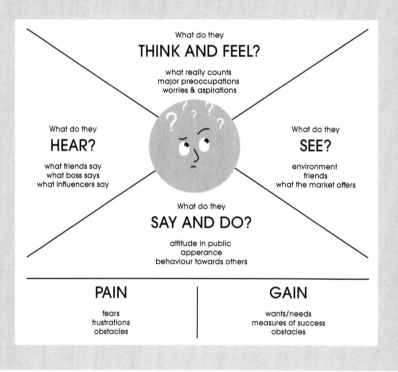

CHAPTER 2

Vulnerability is hard, and it is key

If we are actually going to turn the gender equity and inclusion dial in this generation, then we need to do something fundamentally different. Incredible strides have been taken by our mothers, grandmothers and those who supported them, but it has not created a fast enough momentum in my view. The UN's Sustainable Development Goal 5 is to achieve gender equality by 2030. But at this pace, taking just a couple of examples, it will be the year 2063 before women and men are represented equally in national parliaments, and the year 2280 before we close the gender pay gap.

Sitting in the comfort of the now is just not good enough. My belief is that the difference that will make the difference is our ability as human beings to sit in discomfort, to be able to own our vulnerabilities and see them in ourselves and others as a strength. That way, we can make the changes necessary to create true equity within a reasonable timeframe.

Vulnerability is often misunderstood

For generations, we have heard statements such as 'big boys don't cry', and although this has shifted in recent years and in some geographies, it is still an underpinning subconscious belief that I come across often. It is a masculine trait that is not restricted to men either. When coaching women in leadership roles, it is common for a holding in of emotion to be part of the work. Often, it impacts leaders' abilities to connect and create engagement with their teams, and it is an all-to-familiar occurrence that health (physical and mental) is negatively impacted.

The Reframe

When you consider the dictionary definition of vulnerability, it can be no surprise that the idea of this being our state as a person is something to avoid.

vulnerability

noun

1. the quality or state of being exposed to the possibility of being attacked or harmed, either physically or emotionally.

Emotional vulnerability, though, is more complex. It differs from this literal description, and it has to exist for us to be able to be with those who are different from us.

Emotional vulnerability involves acknowledging how you feel, especially those feelings that are uncomfortable or painful for many

---

of us. It is less about positive emotions like love or joy and more about those unpleasant emotions like anger, shame, anxiety or loneliness.

To be able to change our own behaviours around sex, race, brain functions, religious beliefs and more, we need to first be able to notice our emotions that are connected to them. When we get triggered, upset or offended, being able to own it and name it is an important first step. It is not enough to simply not be sexist or not be racist, for example. We need to sit with our own bias and work on it. We need to take positive steps towards change, and that can only happen if we are willing to be vulnerable. To own our own flaws and failings is something that takes courage. It takes strength and intelligence to be able to know a feeling, articulate it and be willing to learn how to be different.

Tips on how to embrace and build your tolerance of using your vulnerability superpower

1. Get to know yourself. Become aware of what you do and say more consciously.

2. Don't be afraid to ask for help.

3. Share your feelings. Be honest – first with yourself about how you feel.

4. Be in the moment.

5. Set boundaries.

While practising these tips, remember to show yourself compassion. When we practise anything, we fail. It's in the getting back up and going again that we learn and build the muscle. Slow down if you need to and avoid other people's opinions of you.

Complexity, conflict and sitting with the discomfort – developing our inner stance

Anything that involves human beings may be considered complex. We are not complicated creatures or necessarily even difficult (although some may say there are people in their lives who are). What we are is complex because, unlike AI, robots or any form of technology, you cannot know for certain how any one individual will respond in a given situation. You also cannot take for granted that because a person acts in a particular way when something happens, the reaction will be the same on another day with the same stimuli. By living and breathing, we cannot help but have new experiences and learn at an unconscious level each moment we are alive. It may be that existing beliefs are reinforced by our experiences and therefore we hold them more strongly, so react differently. Or it could be that something has happened that gives us a new reference experience that changes how we think and feel about something, and we therefore act in a different way. Even where we have pretty static and steady periods in life, each sunrise and sunset we have the privilege of living through makes for a different day. We are all a different person from the one we were yesterday, down to the very skin we are blessed with.

To create a more inclusive world, it is important that we remember our inbuilt ability to change and grow. Although our brain plasticity changes with age, we can rewire a neural pathway up until the point of death (you can learn more about how to do that in Chapter 3). We create new neural pathways in a split second when major events occur or when we learn something new. So change in a literal sense is absolutely possible. When looking to embrace difference and create equity, we need to figure out and get a sense of the change that will make the difference, then feel the discomfort that the change will inevitably bring and sit with it. All too often in this action-oriented world, we are pushed to act and to act fast. In many situations, this speed to act can be impressive and incredible. It is indeed a useful and valuable skill to have. When it comes to making deeper changes that are about the 'being' part of human being, rather than the knowing or the doing parts, then we must have the ability and resilience to be able to sit with the discomfort long enough to see what emerges. All too often, I notice both in myself and others that the pain of the shift in beliefs and behaviour creates a need to move on, hide or react. The deep-level systemic change that is needed must be allowed the space to come into the light in its own time. Then, when we take action, we can be reassured that we are putting our energy into the real work that is needed and not just dealing with the cracks on the surface.

These deep-level changes are undoubtedly required to move the dial in a meaningful way, and we need to be able to sit with the fact that we are complex beings and that this issue is equally complex. There are so many moving parts, and because life is made up of many people, the dynamics between us are at play. It's okay to not know the answers. It's even okay to get things wrong when we attempt to change. What, in my view, is unforgivable, though, is for us to not even make an attempt to step into the complexity and sit with it, especially when it is uncomfortable, and then, as the right next step emerges, allow ourselves to muster the courage to work through the intra- and inter-relational conflicts that are inevitable in shifts of this depth.

To enable us to unpick some of the complexity of being human, it can be useful to consider Eric Berne's work, which is commonly used in psychotherapeutic settings. The Parent, Adult and Child (PAC) model is a useful way of looking at our behaviours, especially in difficult and challenging situations. It's ideal when you want to work on your own biases, as we are talking about hard and difficult conversations with ourselves and others. Berne differentiates Parent, Adult and Child ego states within the model from being an actual parent, adult or child by the use of a capital. I will do the same here. We look at triggers in a later chapter, and this model enables us to think about where triggers take us. The Parent ego state is when we are running a 'script' that has been imparted and swallowed whole from others – parental or societal norms that we take on as children as how to be. Usually these come from significant others such as parents, caregivers or teachers when we were young. The Adult ego state is where we operate and behave in a way that is appropriate in the here and now.

That does not necessarily mean that you must be behaving in a controlled, considered or positive way – this ego state covers all emotional states from anger to love. For example, it is wholly appropriate in the now if you return home to find you have been burgled for you to be angry or scream and cry. The Child ego state is when we are running a pattern or script from our own younger self, a lived experience that we perceived and made meaning of as a child and carry with us until it is updated.

Consider for a moment where you go when faced with an injustice. Do you hear statements like 'I must…' or 'You should…'? If you do, then know that you may be stepping into the Parent state. The behaviours and energy emitted in Parent will most often call up either other Parent voices or those of the Child. Although these patterns may feel comfortable as they are aligned, they will not create positive change. To enable change for the better, we need to find a way to manage our own state and remain in Adult, even in the face of Parent judgement or Child stomping of feet.

Knowing our preferred position or stance will enable us to navigate the difficulty and conflict more elegantly. Developing our inner Adult stance enables richer conversations to happen and change to occur.

The masculine and the feminine

Specific behaviours or traits are often perceived as either masculine or feminine. I am consciously and deliberately not saying male and female here, not to be clever but to be accurate. This idea is not about gender; it is about the perception of the behaviour. Whereas male or female is used to denote the biological sex of a person, the masculine or feminine is about the attributes that are traditionally associated with each gender. When you consider this, it can come as no surprise that accessing our vulnerability is harder for men or those who associate as masculine. It is also a huge contributor to how the patriarchy is continuing to be upheld – not surprising when you consider the typical descriptions you find when researching the topic.

Common stereotypical attributes include:

Traditional masculine attributes and associations	Traditional feminine attributes and associations
Strong	Caring
Hard	Nurturing
Muscular	Soft
Logical	Emotional
Associated with acquiring wealth, ambition and upholding differentiated gender roles	Associated with collaboration, being in service of and striving for more fluid gender roles

For societal change to happen and inclusion to become the norm, we need to consider vulnerability as a strength and begin to challenge the way we hold the masculine and feminine. An update to the traditional framing and descriptors associated seems a key step towards being able to embrace difference and therefore change the world for the better. If it continues to be understood, often at an unconscious level, that to be masculine you have to be seen as strong and upholding differentiated gender roles, or to be feminine you must not be strong or hard or logical, then the patriarchy will continue to run our experiences.

Story

The moment that I personally tuned into my own relationship with vulnerability and the masculine/feminine sides of me was at a learning group that followed a training in London that looked at personality archetypes. It was around two weeks after the initial weekend course, and we had met up in offices in Marylebone to begin to practise using the new understanding we had in our work. At the time, I was working in a HR management role for a large organisation and had begun my specialism in coaching inside the organisation. Through the exploration of archetype, I recognised that one of my blockers to getting into senior management was part of a pattern, a cycle of behaviour that I had taken on to survive within the traditionally masculine environments in which I had chosen to work. Each day, I chose to actively defeminise how I looked to go to work, unconsciously choosing clothing that would enable me to blend in – greys and creams, hair tied back, and although outwardly confident, most definitely dialled down in terms of offering opinions. Using my intellect to develop reputation while building relationship through task alone became my norm. This meant that I was relying on attributes that held me in a false dualism. I had decided that to succeed I needed to be 'hard', and to be able to be hard you could not therefore be 'soft'. It was a moment I shall never forget when the coach peer I was working with challenged this paradigm with a question about what it might be like to be both hard and soft. In essence, he was asking about vulnerability. It led to my realisation that to grow into becoming a true leader, I would need to embrace this and begin to find ways to live more fully as my whole self in my work. Who wants to be led by someone who only values the hard facts and delivery of task?

Creating psychological safety means people, organisations and societies flourish and thrive

It has been shown through many bodies of research that great leaders create environments that have psychological safety at their heart. This sense of safety enables people to speak up, to share their ideas, and to name the issues and risks.

A psychologically safe environment is one where individuals feel they can ask questions, share new ideas and challenge unethical behaviour without the fear of being punished, embarrassed or rejected.

As leaders, we want our people speaking up about unethical behaviour in the moment so misconduct can be corrected quickly. We also want them to be able to speak out and share their innovative ideas, ask questions and positively challenge others.

The tech giant Google conducted a two-year study on team performance. This revealed that the highest-performing teams have one thing in common: psychological safety – the belief that you won't be punished when you make a mistake. It wasn't about things like how many extroverts or introverts you had in the team or whether you got on socially. It was about trust, equality of voice, and listening in a way that people feel heard – all components of what it takes to build a psychologically safe environment.

> 'In Google's fast-paced, highly demanding environment, our success hinges on the ability to take risks and be vulnerable in front of peers.'
>
> **Paul Santagata**

Other studies have shown that psychological safety allows for moderate risk-taking, speaking your mind, creativity and sticking your neck out without fear of having it cut off – just the types of behaviour that lead to market breakthroughs and truly inclusive cultures in organisations.

Nodding dogs get us nowhere

In essence, we need environments where challenge and support are, in equal measure, the cultural norm. However, we've all sat in those meetings or gatherings where things are simply pleasant. Statements are made, and everyone nods in agreement and often adds in their own version of the same story to reinforce the beliefs in the room. We all like to belong; in fact, it's a core part of our survival instinct as human beings. We are unusual in the mammal world in that when we are born, we cannot fend for ourselves. Unlike cows, elephants and many other mammals, we do not walk moments from birth. This need for others to survive means we are reliant on our tribe, our caregivers, the elders. Without them, we die, so from a very early age, we behave in ways that seek to fit in, to belong, to be looked after and loved. Fast-track from that baby to the adult sitting in a group conversation, and you often find unconscious behaviours at play that seek to fit in. Speaking up when you disagree or have a differing view to offer can be difficult. So what we often experience, especially in organisational settings where there is a set hierarchy and, therefore, power, is what can be referred to as nodding dog syndrome. An echo chamber is created where the boss gives a view, and the team simply agrees or provides evidence and examples that make the boss's view correct. This limits growth at best, and at worst sets things up to fail. Innovation cannot happen without challenging the norm. Norms cannot be challenged unless people feel safe to state a differing view. Simply saying you want others to contribute and that you have an open-door policy is not enough. If you are in a position of power, you have to actively seek out differing opinions. Make sure you invite people with different beliefs and life experiences. Make sure that you actively and visibly encourage and celebrate those who speak up. You need healthy debate to actually happen and people to not just survive but thrive; otherwise, you get a culture that perpetuates and generates the same thing over and over. Encouraging differences of opinion takes courage and patience. You need to be able to listen and really hear what others are saying, even when their views are opposed. A recent example of this for me was during a managers' meeting on-site with a client. We were kicking off a new initiative that focused on the experience of their customers when they come to stores. The topic of diversity and inclusion was one of the four focus areas we were exploring as key to making sure that all people felt welcome and like guests. We were looking at the habits and practices that were the norms in the teams of colleagues and what they may be unconsciously excluding. As we discussed the topic, I offered an observation that in this particular industry, there seemed to be a culture of drinking alcohol being at the core of most team-building activities. I wondered who or how that may be excluding, either for those who have religious beliefs that mean alcohol isn't allowed or who have illnesses like diabetes or alcoholism that make it impossible to join in. As I offered this thought, one of the managers leant back in his chair and said he didn't agree to changing what they currently did as he liked drinking. So in his view, if things changed then he would be excluded. What was brilliant about this start of the debate was that it set a tone that it was okay to be different, it was encouraged to state how you feel, and it enabled me to facilitate a conversation that included all voices to create actions that were focused on true inclusion rather than a 'you're wrong and I'm right' dynamic. It took courage for him, as a white male of a certain age, to say what he felt, and by encouraging the open dialogue, it meant that the team members in the room who were teetotal and/or Muslim were able to offer their ideas for additional team-building activities that didn't include the pub. It was a real 'as well as' exploration and action planning session. The outputs were welcomed more broadly across the team and more people attended events, which has created stronger bonds, and more open and challenging conversations are happening in everyday work situations now.

The farmer and the mechanic

Both farmers and mechanics are hard-working professionals, and both roles require skills and a mindset that puts in effort. When working with leaders across all sectors, I often think of these two examples of ways of operating. The primary difference I notice is that mechanics work on things to fix them, while farmers create environments where things grow through tending to them. When thinking about how we create a psychologically safe work environment that enables people to be at their best, you could arguably take either approach. If you want to change a culture to one that is generative, where difference is valued and equity exists, the farming approach seems to me to be the most useful analogy to keep in mind. Consider the two approaches for a moment and think about which fits with building a world where people can flourish.

Mechanics work on complicated systems. Something is broken or needs fixing, so once it is identified they go about the diagnosis, order in whatever parts might be needed, then install it and you're done. On to the next.

Farmers are working with organic, living material. They don't know what each day might look like as they are continually having to make adjustments because of weather, pests and other unforeseen circumstances. They must continually be paying attention, listening and understanding what is happening in their fields. They put the effort into creating an environment where the crops may flourish – they are not checking each individual carrot!

It seems to me that whether you are leading a family, church, business or sports team, taking the farmer's approach is much more likely to pay dividends. It allows for each part of the 'system' to be itself and change according to the needs of the circumstance rather than looking at each part of the system (children, partner, clergy, employee or management team) as something that needs fixing. Tending the environment is key to growth whenever there are living, complex beings involved.

Systemic principles and constellations

As human beings, we are governed by naturally occurring forces that are set to make sure everything has its place and belongs, that all things have an order, and that things must be in balance to remain effective and vital. Where any one of these gets out of balance in a human system, be it family, business or community, then the system tries to right itself by calling in individuals and groups to correct and find the natural order and balance again. Think of any system as a collection of objects, and a systemic constellation as them standing together to form a pattern. These patterns create a map that illuminates hidden dynamics, things that have got out of order or been forgotten. To make changes in the world around diversity, equity and inclusion, these principles of time, place and balance need to be addressed. Using the idea of representing all elements within the system and creating a map, we are able to get in-depth insights that help establish the source of a problem in a short time. Business (or family) constellations are a great way to tap into the subconscious level and retrieve information that is normally not available to us. They illuminate the hidden dynamics and any loyalties at play within a system. This enables us to broaden our understanding and to sense much more than we would when using other methods. With all things related to diversity, equity and inclusion, it is the hidden, unconscious aspects that hold the current dynamics in place. Gaining an insight into what is really at play can lead to root-cause shifts and a balancing of the system itself.

This way of making change happen is underpinned by some simple truths that have been found to balance successful human systems. The most impactful and arguably key amongst them is that everyone and everything has a 'right place' in their organisational system. Everything must be included, no matter how uncomfortable that may be. Belonging is as strong a human driver as I have known, and to not give someone a place means that energy pushes them to be included. We are tribal beings and have an unconscious need to 'fit'. The purpose, the roles and all the people have a place in each system where they belong (e.g., family, organisation, community), each different but equally valued. When, as individuals or teams, we experience being in the 'right place' systemically, we feel ready to bring our best selves to our role in service of the purpose and can then function with clarity, in flow with the system. It's that sense that all is well, even when being challenged, that enables our full potential to be achieved. Knowing that the effort is worth it and you have a sense of inner congruence and alignment with those around you means that success emerges.

I believe that this deep work could be important in making the fundamental step changes that are needed in the human system that is this world community. Holding the principles of acknowledgement and respect for 'what is' and allowing it to run through your work or life will support you and the people around you to really look at the truths and honour the past before taking a step into the future and on into resolution. Without this we remain stuck in the patterns of old and fighting against the hidden loyalties that exist within us all.

Exercise: Mapping your team – two ways of creating a business constellation

Ideally do this activity with your team to understand how everyone perceives relationships and closeness within the team.

Option one

1. Label a circle with your name and place it in the centre of the table to represent your leadership position.

2. Label additional circles with your team members' names and, using the table edges as the boundary, place these in relation to your name to represent your relationship.

3. Draw arrows on each of your team members' circles. Arrows can point either towards, away from, or be double-ended in relation to your central card, depending on the flow of energy.

4. Capture reflections and lightbulb moments as you are coached through your constellation.

5. Take a photo for your future reference.

Option two

Constellations can also be carried out in a physical way. Each team member physically stands around the leader and their colleagues, positioning themselves at a distance and in a direction that feels right to them based on the issue in question. The aim is to encourage dialogue between each team member, building trust and candour within the team. This can be quite confronting for some people, so I would suggest requesting a facilitator to support you with this exercise.

With this option, it can add real value to have a facilitator from outside the team to make observations and help you notice what's really going on. It is the leader/facilitator's role to ask open-ended and curious questions to support the team members in becoming more aware of the relationships within their constellation, and what they could do to improve connections, if needs be.

Whichever method you choose to go with, it can help to position this approach within the frame of the four ways of knowing. Much of the world now focuses on and gives greater credibility to the intellectual way of knowing things. Over the years, this has led to many of us living in our heads much of the time. Although valuable, it is important to notice that we are more than our brains! There are other ways that we know things. These system-based constellation methods call on the intellect for sure, but it balances this with the other ways that we, as humans, know things. The four ways encompass:

- intuiting and intuitive knowing

- feeling or emotional knowing and emotional intelligence

- embodied knowing

- thinking and cognitive knowing

Our fear of judgement stops us from being our full selves

In my view, the aim of creating more inclusive environments, be they at work or more broadly in society, is to enable each person to bring forth their talents. Imagine what it would be like if each day you were able to relax into being who you are at your heart rather than the societally sculpted version of yourself. When I worked in a corporate environment, at a head office where over a thousand people were based, each morning I used to both feel in an intuitive way and, in my mind's eye, see colleagues walking into the building and leaving a fair chunk of themselves in a skip outside, ready to be collected as they left. This cannot be good for people, for the organisation or for the world!

For many of us, the fear of being rejected or judged runs at a deep level as it is part of the survival instinct of being human. This fear often stops us from being our whole selves or even pushes us into situations where we feel we must hide our truth or else be cast out. Choice is a basic human right, and as I talk about being our whole selves, I am not suggesting that we show every deepest or darkest part to everyone, all of the time. It should be each individual's choice what to show to others rather than being enforced through the team, organisation, community or society. To seek to understand first and then act is a fundamental part of being successful. If we don't get curious, then we are much more likely to make the wrong next move.

Feeling different or excluded stops innovation

Innovation lies in the creative space where we are able to allow ourselves to pause. How often have you found in your life that the great idea comes in the moments when you are doing something mundane, like taking a shower or washing up? Logic might have us believe that genius lies in the focused times when you are in your head, working out the 'answers'. I'd propose a different view, though – being able to relax and let our brains wander and be playful is key to creating something new. This can only happen when you feel safe and the risk of getting it 'wrong' is low. When you feel you are different in some way, whether it's language, race, gender or something as localised as being from a different department in a business within a meeting, you need the environment to be set up in a way that is inclusive for it to feel safe to contribute. Meetings where there are strangers who don't get introduced or where it is unclear as to the part you play in the conversation are perfect examples of where exclusion is created and leads to a lack of contribution and creative thinking. Our brains are less likely to fire off from a place of curiosity, innovation and discovery when our amygdala has been pricked. We need dopamine in our systems to enable clear thinking and engagement. Motivation is the result of the feel-good chemical dopamine, and survival instincts kick in when cortisol floods through us if there is fear, which shuts us down.

We are hardwired to notice things in our environments that are threats. So to create an environment where all can bring their A game, we need to actively and consciously find ways to play to the positive and set us up for a dopamine hit.

Blame is fear being discharged

When we have experienced judgement, it often creates patterns of belief that play out throughout our lives. It is comfortable because of its familiarity, but its impact also creates pain and discomfort. When things go wrong, it is all too easy to immediately go to the question, 'Whose fault is this?' Seeking out someone to blame gives us a sense of being in control. When you are on the receiving end of blame or find yourself caught in a gossip space, know that these are indicators of a judgemental environment. Where judgement exists, you are most likely to find 'in' crowds and 'out' crowds. These behaviours form the basis of exclusion and are the antithesis of an inclusive culture. It takes real vulnerability and strength when things go wrong to notice the part we might have played or to be curious about what needs to happen to make things better without getting stuck in the blame game. We have to hold ourselves accountable and notice what's really going on. To err is human, so we must forgive ourselves when we get things wrong and stop ourselves from making it someone else's fault. The first step has to be to catch ourselves in the moment when we are tempted to rage for 15 seconds to discharge the fear and discomfort. Finding more healthy ways to get a sense of control and groundedness is more likely to create growth and encourage equity in any culture.

When you come across blamers or gossips in a work context, know that the first thing to do is stop yourself colluding with the behaviour. Step back and show empathy. Then ask questions that are solution-focused, questions that help move the conversation from the problem and into accountability and ownership. Asking 'What outcome are you after and how will you know you've got it?' is more likely to enable a person to step into their own power.

Judgement is a protection and often a reflection of ourselves

In judgement, we find safety. It's where we can hide out and make certain that we never have to change things ourselves. By making others 'wrong' and protecting myself in the 'right', it feels like I can stay on top and in control. Many people judge when they feel judged by others or even themselves. At its heart, judgement is a form of self-defence. Freud would say that judgement is a means of protecting our fragile egos. We project the attitudes, desires, behaviours and thoughts that we don't like in ourselves onto others, who we then judge. In this way, we can disassociate from the very thing in ourselves that secretly we might most want to be different.

Being judgemental is different from passing judgement. We all make judgements. It is a completely appropriate way to discern and evaluate your actions and direction of travel. Discernment and evaluation are about using information to make wise decisions. For example, asking yourself, 'Does this employee demonstrate the necessary skills for a promotion?' is a way of making a judgement that is our right and responsibility. Inequity arises when these judgements become judgemental and are therefore loaded with stereotypes, assumptions and generalisations. If you start answering the 'Do they have the skills?' question with things like 'They have small children, so as a mum they won't be able to commit the hours needed' or 'Women always/never…' statements, then hit the pause button immediately. Once paused, consider what else might be true and capture the question you need answering to know if they have the skills required. Then ask them or alternatively bin the question if you notice it is irrelevant to the decision. (e.g., When did the hours we work affect the skills we bring? Bin it.)

The next time you find yourself being judged by someone, it is useful to remember that it's a reflection of their own battle with shame and not what or who you are. Leave the thoughts, feelings and statements where they belong – with the judger.

> 'Don't take anything personally. Nothing others do is because of you. What others say and do is a projection of their own reality, their own dream. When you are immune to the opinions and actions of others, you won't be the victim of needless suffering.'
> **Don Miguel Ruiz**

The independence myth can get you stuck

Independence is a myth that can often be used to justify defending ourselves against actually connecting with others and the risk of being hurt. It is a common trait that I experience being an overused strength most with women, and I have to say that I personally only began to let go of this myth in my mid-thirties. The moment I clocked that I was actually damaging myself and my relationships is as clear in my mind today as it was 15–20 years ago when it happened. My cab had pulled up outside of the hotel I was staying at in Scotland, where I was attending a three-day conference for work. I had my right arm in a sling due to an ongoing injury that had torn the nerves and ligaments in my shoulder. As I got out of the cab, the driver followed and offered to get my bags out of the boot and carry them inside. My instinctive reaction was to say 'No thank you' and to attempt to get them out myself with my one good arm! In that split second, I recognised that I was running a pattern of behaviour that had once upon a time enabled me to leave difficult situations and relationships that were, on reflection, controlling and coercive. They were in my past, though, and I was now playing out the pure independent woman 'I can do it all myself' role to the detriment of me and those I loved. My reference point needed a long-overdue update.

As human beings, we are gloriously interdependent. We need each other to both survive and thrive. Yet society's emphasis on independence can cause shame. It creates internal struggles that many of us face when the option of asking for help rears its head. Just think of the phrase I heard often as a child: 'God helps those who help themselves.' It's an example of the kind of messaging that tells us clearly what is expected, even for those of us who aren't particularly religious. We are told that asking for help is seen as a weakness. I now know this to be an untruth. Needing help makes us human. It's a win-win situation when we ask for help because it can be a really satisfying and uplifting feeling for those giving the help. To be of use and to make someone else's day easier somehow creates a sense of contentment that is hard to replicate in any other way. We all have different strengths and weaknesses, so matching and finding ways to use each other's strengths is a wonderful way of balancing the universe.

I was reminded recently of how important it is for those of us who have influence in our lives, whether it's through a leadership role, our place in our community or parenthood, to make sure that we show others how to ask for help. In a management meeting I was recently facilitating, one of the senior managers was talking about the stress levels within the organisation and how he had been telling his team to ask for help. He was shocked that, even though he said this to his team regularly, no one was asking for help, and instead they were starting to see burnout amongst team members and some unhealthy working practices emerge. In almost the same breath, when asked about how he was managing in the current pressured climate, he said that he puts his head down and pushes through the workload. A lightbulb came on metaphorically in the room at that point as his peers noticed, and named, that he was telling his team to do one thing (ask for help), and he was doing the exact opposite (not asking for help). Teams and families alike will mirror the acceptable behaviours that they see and experience and not what they are told to do. As Ghandi so wisely once said: 'Be the change you want to see in the world.'

Overused strengths can be our Achilles heel

I believe that understanding our strengths and being able to own them is an important part of being an adult. For those of us raised in cultures where it is seen as 'in poor taste' to talk about what you are good at, the result is often false modesty. This need to fit the societal norm seems to impact women in the workplace more than others. Studies have shown that men are much more likely to say 'I' when referencing a positive that has happened and 'we' when something has gone wrong. For women, the opposite is true. This means that at a subliminal level, we are telling all that we don't achieve things, even when we are leading the team (e.g., 'It was a team effort'), while also setting ourselves up to take full responsibility for the errors or failures (e.g., 'I will get on to this straight away').

Consider some of the key strengths that we bring to our work and lives and how they play out when overused. The impact these have can be catastrophic, and often this creates a knee-jerk reaction to 'fixing', which entails cutting the behaviour out. Where an overused strength is the cause of the issue, though, we do not want to stop. We need to aim to dial it down instead.

Supportive becomes Self-Sacrificing	Risk-Taking becomes Reckless	Persevering becomes Stubborn
Loyal becomes Blind	Ambitious becomes Ruthless	Reserved becomes Distant
Trusting becomes Gullible	Self-Confident becomes Arrogant	Cautious becomes Suspicious

We must aim to notice what is happening, be courageous enough to name it and then take action with others' support if we want to break through the challenges faced in creating diverse and inclusive teams. It is much easier to take on board feedback that names the strength first. For example, you could say, 'I really value your trusting nature in the team as it makes new starters on the project feel at ease and welcome. They are then more productive and faster. There are times when your strength can be perceived as gullible, though, as you aren't doing due diligence when taking in work from other departments. This is leading to us having to rework tasks.' That's much more likely to be heard than, 'You are too trusting and gullible. You take other departments' work at face value, and it's making us have to do rework too often.' It makes sure the person knows the change that's needed is to dial it down, NOT to stop trusting.

Social norming and the need to think, *F*** conformity*

Self-concept plays an important role in conformity to sex-typed social norms. Normative behaviours, including that men are powerful, dominant and self-assertive and that women are caring, intimate with others and emotionally expressive, set a standard that we often hold without consciously choosing. Although these are changing as each generation challenges the status quo, there is still too prevalent a sense of these being upheld across education and the workplace. Just yesterday, I was having a conversation with a senior manager within an organisation I work with – let's call him Jack – who shared that their four-year-old son loves crafting. The little boy had been making a bracelet with sparkly beads and dolphins, and once finished had said to Jack that this is for Mummy. Jack said how much he loved the bracelet and that he would love to wear it. When he asked if it could be for Daddy, not Mummy, his son replied, 'Boys don't wear sparkles, Daddy, and it's pink so it has to be for a girl.' Jack was stunned and concerned as to where this bias had been learned as he is an advocate across his sector for equity and diversity, so he actively makes sure that home is equal. He and his wife do 50/50 childcare, and both work. They are very consciously creating a gender-neutral environment. It clearly shows that societal norming is alive and well, as these beliefs were being picked up through nursery, playgroups or the broader family.

For us to truly effect equality at work, we need to find ways to challenge and change norms. We are social creatures, and it is an unchangeable truth that we will step into herd mentalities, so how do we find ways to change the narrative and make the norm one of inclusion? I'd say a great start for each of us, and especially those in positions of authority, whether formal or informal, would be to start to question everything better. Actively do the opposite or something different from the 'norm'. Demonstrate and encourage different approaches and ideas. Challenge stuck thinking with kindness and empathy, but make sure you are heard.

Understanding social norming – the Asch experiment

Asch's theory posits that people conform to the opinions of others when they perceive that their group membership or social identity is at stake. To test his theory, Asch conducted a series of experiments that involved participants answering simple questions about the length of lines on a piece of paper. Each participant was placed in a group with several other group members who were actually staff/actors who had been told what to answer. In each trial, the group were asked to say which of the lines was the same length as the standard line. The correct answer was obvious, and the task was designed so that the staff/actors would give obviously incorrect answers. This meant that the person who was a true participant rather than staff/actor had a choice as to whether to give the correct answer or follow the group with the incorrect answer.

In the first few trials, the participants generally gave correct answers. However, very quickly they began to give incorrect answers. Asch found that around 75% of the real participants conformed to the group's incorrect answer at least once, and about one-third conformed in more than 50% of the trials. He also noted that as the group size got bigger, the chance of conforming rose so that around four out of five would conform with the group's incorrect answer. Conformity was higher when the group were unanimous in their opinion, and conformity was lower when participants had at least one ally who gave the correct answer.

Asch's conformity theory has far-reaching implications when you think of the impact on creating equity, embracing difference and changing the world. His findings show that individuals are highly influenced by the opinions of others, especially if their social identity is at stake. Imagine the impact on decision-making in groups around things like who to recruit, pay and reward! Individuals may be hesitant to express their true opinions if they fear rejection or exclusion from the group themselves. The importance of having an ally in the room when you are in the minority is really clear. This is why gender equity, for instance, is not a women's issue. It takes all genders to step out of the social norming that is in place within the patriarchy. This runs deeper, too, as his theory helps us understand how individuals form attitudes and beliefs. They often form them based on the opinions of those around them. Think about if an individual is surrounded by people who hold strong political views and beliefs as an example. They are much more likely to adopt those beliefs themselves. It's pure socialisation. Considering and consciously choosing who we surround ourselves with and how we show up as an ally is the only way to shift the dial and break the norm.

Exercise: How to change your neural pathways and break out of the norm

Changing neural pathways? What am I on about? Well, neuroplasticity is the brain's ability to reorganise itself by forming new neural pathways throughout life and in response to experiences. While the brain usually does this itself in response to injury or disease, when humans focus their attention enough, they can slowly rewire these pathways themselves. Every new experience has the potential to enhance your brain's ability to change.

So to break the social norming patterns that will have set the pathways in your brain unconsciously until now, here are some experiences you could choose to have that could promote neuroplasticity and enable a more inclusive way of living:

1. Take new routes

Whether it's in and around your neighbourhood or further afield, travelling can help. Our brains are forced to stop auto-piloting in an unfamiliar environment like a new city or when we wander off the normal routes we take to familiar places.

Research by Elsevier B.V. from 2013 shows that novelty and challenges can enhance cognitive function. So, technically, you don't even have to leave your town to promote brain plasticity.

Consider finding alternative routes to your daily commute. Try that new coffee shop or restaurant around the corner. Go around your desk in the opposite direction to the one you typically follow.

2. Move

Recent research has shown that physical exercise can promote neuroplasticity in general. Many different regions of the brain are positively affected by us being active. Activity affects various aspects of cognitive function, including memory and learning. Exercising may help you slow the cellular ageing process and enhance your overall brain health. Healthier brains make better decisions.

3. Practise meditation

We've touched on this earlier in this book, and here I want to connect it to the impact it has on the neural pathways we lay down. Studies show that meditation can change the function of the brain. Specifically, mindfulness practice can enhance focus and attention.

4. Learn something new

The relationship between learning and neuroplasticity is twofold. Learning new things enhances brain plasticity, and because of the brain's ability to adapt to change, you're able to learn. It's a real win-win situation and one of the reasons I'm a massive advocate for having a lifelong learner mindset. Every time you learn something, you benefit from neuroplasticity and promote it, so why wouldn't you want that, no matter how old you are?

So pick up that paintbrush and learn to paint in watercolours, speak a new language, play a new instrument, take up a new sport, do puzzles, write with your non-dominant hand – the list is endless and the learning doesn't need to be hard. Have some fun with it.

5. Rest

A lack of sleep seems to contribute to a decrease in neurogenesis, the process that allows the brain to repair and change. Research shows that not getting enough sleep inhibits the body's capacity for neuroplasticity. For those of us with either a neurodivergence ourselves or children with a neurodiversity like autism or ADHD, this one can be tricky. In our household so far this week, we have had three nights where our 12-year-old has been walking the corridors until 2am because he is just not tired. His record was during lockdown when the loss of routines and uncertainty increased his anxiety, and he managed three days straight without one wink of sleep. During that time, there was little rest for my husband or me as we tag-teamed to stay with him to ensure safety.

Whatever approach you decide to take to creating new pathways and building neuroplasticity, know that each time you practise some of the above you are enabling your brain to flex more easily. Your ability to make different choices increases – important skills when wanting to embrace difference.

CHAPTER 3

Call out bad behaviour (with empathy)

It's all too easy to shrug off the small everyday things that we encounter. Sometimes, we don't notice them because they are 'just the way things are', and at other times it may feel like a battle not worth fighting. There is a spectrum of emotion that can come when something like everyday sexism happens (for sexism, you could as easily read racism, judgement of neurodiversity or homophobic comments). Much of the time, statements or comments seem harmless, but they reinforce in a quiet way the patriarchy within the system. As I write this book, I am noticing I have a heightened awareness of my everyday language and a curiosity about its impact. So the other day when I heard myself use the term 'bigwigs' in conversation with another coach, I hit the pause button, stopped and said to her, 'I wonder what the root of the word is?' She immediately looked it up, and the expression originated in the 1700s, and it is indeed literal. In the 17th and 18th centuries, many European noblemen wore big wigs to showcase their wealth or significance in society. In those days, wigs were very expensive to acquire and keep in good condition. It's a subtle but nonetheless effective way for me to hold the truth in the system and normalise that the men are in power with the added touch that it's also the monied who call the shots! As you can imagine, I have now struck this from my phrasebook unless I am specifically working in the legal field and referencing history.

Step up and step in

The example of old phrases is a safe space to begin noticing and calling ourselves and others to account. It still takes courage as none of us want to be seen as overly sensitive or picky. It's important to make the small changes as they are endemic in society and hold the current system in place. More overt situations may involve work colleagues or family/friends acting in ways that a few decades ago were socially acceptable but today are not okay. Some of my work takes me into the automotive industry, and this is where I still see the most obvious examples of this dated behaviour. I must say it's not exclusive to this industry, and many diversity, equity and inclusion awards are being given to some organisations in this industry, a great example being the work through the 30% Club. Back to the examples, though, as they are hidden in plain sight most often. Here are a few of the stories from a recent series of conversations and focus groups I held:

A female car salesperson came back from a test drive that took around 30 minutes longer than average. She had spent the time to really understand the customer's needs and had sold him a vehicle that was £20k more expensive as it matched his requirements. Instead of congratulating her or asking how she had done it, her male colleagues joked that she must have pulled into a lay-by with him to convince him! She shrugged it off and let it slide as it was a regular occurrence and labelled as harmless banter. Let's be clear, though, that if she had been a male salesperson, this wouldn't have even been thought about, much less said out loud. Sexual innuendo is never okay, no matter how well intended or if it is done without thought.

In a resource-stretched car service team, they had been trying to recruit a new supervisor for the front desk. The manager had been in conversation with the current workshop controller as they felt he would be well-suited. One of the female service advisers had attempted to demonstrate her ability to step into the role by 'acting up' and taking on tasks outside of her job role. She had, earlier in her career, been in a managerial position in another store. These facts were known to the manager, but she hadn't been spoken with about the role. After conversation, I uncovered an underlying and unconscious assumption that the manager had running that led to his behaviour. As the adviser had just had a baby in the last year, he hadn't considered her because his belief was that she wasn't interested in her career now. He hadn't had a conversation with her about her aspirations and had put her on the 'mummy track' in his head. If he had taken the time to have the conversation with her, he would have learned that her partner had made the choice that they would be a stay-at-home dad, and she was fully focused on learning, growing and building a career.

A number of young women in the team across departments were spending an inordinate amount of time each morning considering what they would wear so that they weren't open for comments. Things like 'You should wear that skirt more often as it's nice to see your legs' made the women cautious to the extent that they wore flat shoes and trousers every day. These conversations were illuminating to the director I was working with, and he was shocked as he believed he had a real sense of connection and family feel in the culture of the organisation. The stories we heard went against his personal values in the extreme, and he wanted to act immediately. He had the courage to step up and step in, so we called a managers meeting and shared a clear and explicit set of behavioural expectations. With the women's permission, we offered some real-life examples to bring things home and enable the broader team to understand specifically what wasn't okay and what was. By empowering both men and women to name what was happening and say it wasn't okay, a huge and fast change has occurred on-site, with those who were unwilling to see the need for change, let alone do something different, opting to work elsewhere.

The what, the why and the how of courage

It takes time, energy and courage to step up and step in. Deciding it matters enough for you to change something, either within yourself or where others are acting in a way that is not okay, is the first step, but without action it's meaningless. To me, courage is the moment you make the decision to speak up when you are pretty certain that you will not be greeted with open arms or ears. Why courage is so key is something that, to me, seems so apparent that it almost doesn't need naming. However, I have learned that unless you are explicit about what you mean, things can go off on rather unexpected tangents. For me, the why is because without courage, nothing changes, and change is needed now. Without change, individuals who are 'different' and families, like mine, who aren't matching the societal behavioural norms will continue to be excluded. The penalty for this exclusion is not only the pain and isolation caused to the person and family, which can be extraordinarily high, but the cost of the loss of talent to the world. Without the creative brains of those who are neurodivergent, we cannot expect to solve the Earth-threatening challenges that are currently being faced, be they economic or environmental. Without the feminine and the masculine equally in balance in the system that is our universe, the world will remain off-kilter.

When you are in the minority, it takes a special kind of courage to speak up, and the great news is that courage is a skill that can be learned.

The word 'courage' may mean different things to each person. We will also all apply it in different ways because, for some of us, certain things take courage that for others are easy. For instance, it takes a huge amount of courage for me to handle heights. So when recently I was at a conference centre where the only access point was via a raised walkway, it took massive energy and courage for me to get across and into the building, whereas the colleague I was with strolled over without a thought. By the time we got to the room where we were facilitating our session for the day, I found myself needing to take a moment away from the team to regroup after the adrenalin rush of my response to the height issue. You cannot assume when courage might be needed or shown. Just be open to the impact and the time that may be needed to regroup.

To be able to be open-minded, it's important to explore what courage means for you and to show empathy when its need may show up for others.

I believe that researcher and storyteller Brené Brown captures the best explanation of what courage is:

'Courage – the original definition of courage, when it first came into the English language, is from the Latin word cor, *meaning heart and the original definition was to tell the story of who you are with your whole heart.'*

This idea of courage being wholehearted and of us stepping into our true selves really resonates with me. I believe it may be the only way to create equity, diversity and inclusion in our world. Remember that equity isn't about making those who have privilege feel or act smaller – it's about having an environment and culture that enables all to be themselves with equal opportunities on a level playing field. Courage enables us to notice realities, to sit with the discomfort and then to lean in and take action to change things in a way that respects all.

Courage takes practice. It means keeping your eyes and ears open for opportunities to positively affect your environment and the people in it.

Exercise: Courage self-audit

Conversation or reflection 1

Think back to when you were a bright young thing at the beginning of your career. (Career may be in the working world or it may be as a homemaker or other non-organisational activity.)

- How did you show courage?

- How did you get your ideas heard?

- When blockers happened, what were they, and how did you overcome them?

Conversation or reflection 2

Now stepping back into the present and from your seat as manager/educator/parent/carer of today's bright young things.

- What can you do to remove blockers?

- What blockers may you be creating or colluding with?

- What can you now change in your way of working/behaving that would make things easier for the upcoming generation?

- How might you share what worked for you?

Use your privilege to good effect

The word privilege can be a trigger for many when on the receiving end of being labelled as such. Especially for those of us who grew up on council estates or in poverty, the idea of being privileged is counter to our lived experience. The challenge here is to allow yourself to truly consider what privilege really is, because it isn't money. Money can buy privileged access to many things like private education or a network of mentors and support that helps you throughout your career. Money doesn't buy all privilege, though.

When you think of the meaning of the word privilege as having any right, immunity or benefit enjoyed only by a person or group beyond the advantages of most, then your thinking may change.

Here are some examples of privilege, some of which you will be aware of and others you may not have considered as privilege before:

- Environmental privilege – You do not live in an area that's within one mile of the landfill dump.

- White privilege – You can walk into any supermarket and find the staple foods that fit with your cultural traditions or into a hairdresser's shop and find someone who can cut your hair.

- Able-bodied privilege – You don't make people uncomfortable by just existing.

- Heterosexual privilege – You can be open about your sexual orientation without worrying about your job.

- Male privilege – If you have children and pursue a career, no one will think you're selfish for not staying at home.

- Christian privilege – You can expect to have time off work to celebrate your religious festivals like Easter and Christmas.

Unless you have lived a life or spent time with people who are different from you, then you may not even have an awareness of the privileges you have. Things may simply feel 'normal' to you, and if you've stepped back to look at things, you may even have assumed that everyone has the same opportunity because that's what you experience. I can never know what it is like to live in an area where the colour of my skin dictates others' reactions to me. What I can reference is my lived experience of being the adoptive parent of a child with ADHD and autism. When I compare the challenges we face to be able to complete simple daily tasks like popping to get some milk, booking a trip during the school holidays or being able to eat outside on a sunny day, then the playing field is definitely not level. Until living it, though, I would never have known the challenges or the creative thinking and risk-taking that are needed just to function and grasp a sliver of 'normal' family life. To illustrate this for you, here are a few examples of what families like ours need to be ready for and plan as best we can to manage so we can get by. The list highlights the topic but not the depth of detail required and is definitely not exhaustive, as each family will be different depending on needs:

- **Booking a family holiday**: Loud noises first thing in the morning and stimming activities like stomping mean we need a soundproofed space – so a whole home and not a flat, tent or hotel room. We prefer space where there will not be other children of a similar age as we need regulation space with no 'missing out' on playing. We need to run through the social story (photos/videos) of new places a few times leading up to the trip. We avoid shops and stops while travelling as each one can cause overwhelm and a meltdown – some petrol station stops have been known to take 40 minutes, and we've even had a milkshake-throwing meltdown at Starbucks on the A30. Trips are easier if we have been there before. Packing requires many more outfits than you may need, especially of the costume variety – we currently need to pack around three different styles of Spiderman outfits and a Harry Potter one as they are the favoured films of the moment, which can only be watched if dressed appropriately. This is also true with football kits and playing FIFA or watching a match on TV.

- **Travelling to family/friends**: We need to make sure there is either internet access or downloaded shows/games for the duration of the trip to aid regulation and avoid the need to stop en route. We can only share that the trip is happening shortly before going to avoid the anxiety of worrying that he has missed it. We can only stay with friends/family who can be accepting of the therapeutic way that you need to parent and who can keep the atmosphere light, even in difficulties. We share a 'my story' style sheet to let them know what the current triggers are – for example, for our little guy, having his photo taken is an issue that can cause a meltdown. Where there are other children, we are unlikely to stay over, so we need to go on day trips or find local accommodation. Friends and family also need to be educated about what is needed and likely to happen with everyday things like bedtimes.

- **Family outings to activity places like Legoland, etc.**: We have to contact the accessibility team prior to the visit to arrange carer tickets so that the cost is bearable should we need to leave within a few minutes because it's too much. We also need social stories, including photos, videos and maps to show before going. Queuing is not an option for us, so we have to find out what extra documentation we need to get a fastpass for certain areas or rides and arrange it all beforehand – waiting on the day will use up some of the processing capacity that a neurodiverse brain has and often means that we cannot stay. We plan Blue Badge parking near the entrance so that we can make a quick exit if necessary.

- **Getting to school**: If walking, we make every 50 yards a target with a fun game or race involved. If driving, we leave plenty of time for the transition out of the house, as this is particularly difficult. 'Practising' in the run-up to going back to school after the holidays is necessary to normalise it again. (Having a specialist-setting school or mainstream that understands the challenges of the transitions needed just to get to school makes this whole thing so much more manageable.) If we are late, we don't want to do the 'walk of shame' to get to the classroom with our already anxious child and need to be able to arrive dressed as Superman or Ronaldo if that's who he needs to feel like to get there.

- **Buying food essentials**: We do everything in our power to make sure we don't need to pop to the shops. Every trip is laden with potential overwhelm, meltdowns and a need to feed the impulsivity that comes, for some, with neurodiversities like ADHD.

- **Ordering something online**: If you are ordering something for someone with a neurodiversity, then make sure that you take the next-day delivery option wherever possible. The time blindness associated with the diversity can bring with it huge anxiety. Our son, when awaiting a delivery, holds it in mind almost constantly and needs to check with us many times each day to ask if it's here yet. Each time, we then need to go through the counting process of how many sleeps and show him on the calendar. Often, marking off on a calendar as a visual aid can help, but avoiding the challenge altogether is the best plan.

Not all families that have children or adults with additional needs will have these exact experiences, but I can be certain that many will have some or all and others that we do not have. Consider this in your working life: How differently would you treat the colleague sitting next to you if you knew that they had spent the first couple of hours of their morning with their child screaming and threatening them or throwing things in an autistic meltdown? Or consider what you could do differently to enable a team member to fully engage and be able to contribute in meetings if you knew how much energy it took for them to simply sit still.

Staying safe – choosing your battles matters

To change the world to become more inclusive is an important intention, and I am an advocate for speaking up. It is also necessary to be able to hold back when the impact you might have could put you or others in harm's way, when it could exacerbate an already volatile situation, or when the energy you would need to expend would have little to no impact. Putting yourself in danger, either physically, professionally or psychologically, is not the way to approach this. We need long-term, sustainable actions to achieve the kind of shift that will make a systemic difference.

Sometimes it is best to say less

This is a hard-won lesson for many of us – me included. As someone who is led by my values and who believes in justice, it has been a habit over the years to step in and be the voice that names the difficulty or challenges the situation. Often, this has been a reactive response, usually in defence of others, and although noble, it is not always effective or sometimes even welcome. There are times when you are not best placed to be the voice of change or challenge. The cost personally may be too high. Dodging the bullets that come back when you step into the battle can be ill-timed and dangerous. An example for me was after an 18-month battle with the education services to get a place in a specialist school provision for my autistic and ADHDer son. His current school had informed us that they could no longer meet his needs and that meant he would not have a school place in the very near future. He was at risk of permanent exclusion, even though they knew that his behaviour was due to his disability, and the reality was that they could not provide what he needed to be able to manage in a school setting. The fight to get the place took tenacity, resilience and resources that I feel privileged to have. Imagine having to have to push back and get the director of Child Services involved in your case, to need to call every specialist provision in the county to understand provision scope and place availability (or waiting list length), let alone understand if you felt that the school was a good fit culture-wise for your family or the travel for drop off and pick up fitted with your working schedule. I had to learn a whole new language along with all the acronyms so that the council's department of education and the schools would listen and understand. I had to get educational psychologist reports and assessment after assessment to prove the level of need. I had to do all this while also being the parent of a child with complex additional needs. After winning the personal battle and getting him a place at a school that could meet his needs to be able to access an education, I had the bit between my teeth and wanted to take on the whole system – to get to Parliament and change the way policy was made and resourcing was funded. I started pulling together a team to affect things at a local and national level. It was not okay that the very families who needed the most support were the ones having to give up the most to get basic needs met. During a coaching supervision call, I was rightly challenged on my drive to make these changes. Exploring where my energy was most needed made me step back and notice that although I had a passion for change and a desire to support other parents in this situation, my husband and son needed me back. They hadn't had my energy for nearly two years as I had been expending so much in my quest to get our needs met by the system. The battle to take on the world wasn't mine for now. I needed to take a pause as the cost of leaning in would have been too much. Finding ways to affect the system without breaking my own was the only sustainable approach.

Boundaries and assumptions

To be boundaryless or boundary blind can lead to burnout, lack of fulfilment and a sense of being lost, overlooked or taken advantage of. Our relationship with boundaries is one that needs to be observed, sat with and then crafted to make sure that we are holding them in a way that is strong without strangulation. No one can tell you what your boundaries need to be, but if you have not identified and articulated what they are to others, then you have very little hope of them being upheld or respected. An example that is true for me became really highlighted when we took the decision as a family to move out of London. I found that the number of nights I spent staying away from home for work had got to a level where I felt guilty, detached from what was happening with my husband and son, and sad to be missing out. My inner turmoil about what was happening hit a high when I was regularly away for four nights a week. This was a breaking point for me to realise that when we moved I hadn't set myself a boundary on travel. I tested my thinking and landed on the fact that my ideal was two nights away maximum, with the occasional third night if the work was something I was particularly passionate about or the client was one that I adored working with. This setting of the boundary doesn't mean that on occasion I don't breach it, but when I do it is now a conscious act, and the discomfort I feel around it holds me in check so that it won't become a habit.

When it comes to creating inclusive cultures and spaces to make sure our needs are met, we must be aware of not only our boundaries but also the assumptions that we will have running about other people's boundaries. Assumptions occur because we are social beings who make meaning and see patterns, so we map across our experiences and generalise to make sense of the world and make it easier to navigate. If our brains didn't filter the way we explored in the last chapter, then we would be in a state of near-constant overwhelm. Assumptions about boundaries based on our own opinions of what is appropriate, good or bad in specific circumstances can rarely be accurate and most likely end up in excluding or judging others in an unhelpful way. How can we possibly know others' boundaries and needs without asking?

To change the world, we need to ask questions and call out 'bad' behaviour, and yet, I wonder, who sets what is bad and what is good? For many of us, it is societal norms and our upbringing that dictate what we assume is appropriate. Depending on the generation in which we were raised, this will have a big impact. What was okay in 1980 is very different from what was okay in 1950 or indeed in 2023. When I think back to my mum's generation, her mum's and mine, compared to my son's and goddaughters', what was possible for girls and women or those who are different has changed immensely. It would have been considered 'bad' in my mum's youth not to aspire to become a wife and mother in your twenties. For many, it felt like the only choice. In Victorian England, the second you got married as a woman, everything you owned became your husband's, and you had to give up work. So what was bad and good was very different.

To make sure we are calling out the behaviours that will make the difference, we first need to audit our own thinking and assumptions on what is taken as a given, what we consider bad or an 'obvious' boundary that we all need, and then consciously decide what needs to shift to create the culture that we want to create. If we were to fly out 20 years into the future, what will we need to experience to know that things have changed in the way we wish? To clearly be able to see and experience that equity is the norm, certain things will be happening around us. Our aim has to be that people in future generations look back and see this as another turning point in society's growth. In whatever part of the world you live or whatever field you work, be it education, community or business, what are the specifics that will be on the list of 'normal' that tell you that equity exists? What now feels as easy as breathing but used to feel like a fight? Important questions for us all to ponder and answer.

Exercise: Changing the way we feel, think and therefore behave

Setting healthy boundaries and holding them requires us first to believe that we are worth the effort and the outcome that they will provide. Sometimes our underpinning beliefs are based on our lived experiences, and at other times they are based on current societal norms. Either way, they are held in not only the brain but also the body, and to change them requires us to do more than simply think differently. Below is a submodality belief change tool that gets you into the deeper level way that we code things in our whole system. By shifting one element at a time, you can check what works for you and what makes it better or, indeed, worse. The most powerful thing here is to recognise that you are in charge of how you hold information and what you feel. It's your mind and your body, so feel free to make the shifts you desire to feel different in any given circumstance.

So what are submodalities? They are subsets of the modalities (visual, auditory, kinaesthetic, olfactory, gustatory and auditory digital) that are part of each representational system. Submodalities give us a way to change limiting beliefs into empowering ones.

Sub

Below; under; beneath: *subsoil.*

a. Subordinate; secondary: *subplot.*

b. Subdivision: *subregion.*

Mode

A manner, way, or method of doing or acting: *modern modes of travel.*

A particular form, variety, or manner: *a mode of expression.*

A tendency to conform to a general pattern or belong to a particular group.

Here's how to change a submodality belief:

1. Select the limiting belief you want to change. Limiting beliefs are most easily identified by thinking about the things you would like to achieve but aren't currently working towards. Then look at your justification for why you aren't working towards them. This story we tell ourselves will be the root of the limiting belief. Common limiting beliefs include: I don't have time, I don't have what it takes, I'm not strong enough, and I don't deserve it.

2. Elicit all submodalities in detail (see table opposite for a list of the submodalities to consider by sense).

3. Now think of some other positive experience and belief that is true for you. Elicit the submodalities of this state.

4. Now think of the preferred belief that you want to have instead of that #1 limiting belief.

5. Do a map across from Step #2 belief to Step #1. You have to map across from the belief that is true for you to the belief that you will prefer to lose.

6. As you change each submodality, make a note of whether it is better, worse or neutral (use tables opposite). If it's better, then leave it; if it's worse or neutral, then change it back to the original.

7. Once you have worked through the submodalities, notice first what feels different and then test: What is your belief now? If you see positive change, keep it; if not, repeat the process.

Negative experience

Submodalities	Worse	Neutral	Better
Visual			
Distance			
Colour			
Movie/still			
Auditory			
Location			
Pitch			
Tempo			
Kinaesthetic/Feel			
Temperature			
Pressure			
Location			

Positive experience

Submodalities	Worse	Neutral	Better
Visual			
Distance			
Colour			
Movie/still			
Auditory			
Location			
Pitch			
Tempo			
Kinaesthetic/Feel			
Temperature			
Pressure			
Location			

Staying safe and taking risks

We all have a different appetite for risk, and we all have a different experience of the world when it comes to safety. This struck home for me just last week when I was on a business trip to Birmingham. It was a glorious evening when I pulled into New Street Station on the train, and looking at Google Maps I could see that my hotel was only a 15-minute walk. I adore walking and getting to know places I visit and have found over the years that strolling through the streets and looking up to take in the architecture is a great way to do that. So off I set, pulling my suitcase behind me. About three or four minutes' walk out of the station, I started to feel an odd sensation and then noticed the number of people begging for money around me. I then looked at the entirety of the walk on the map, zooming in on the satellite view, and realised that there was a long subway that I would need to take to get to the part of the city where I was staying. As a woman walking alone, it did not feel safe to continue, so I walked back to the station and got a taxi. I mentioned this experience to my husband when I got home the following day, as it had really stayed with me. At first, he looked confused, and when I asked more it became clear that this wasn't something he'd ever had to consider. If he wants to walk, he just does – safety isn't a consideration. This experience got me thinking about the who and the how when it comes to shifting cultural norms and the behaviours that hold the current dynamics in place. Without everyone involved, no matter how they identify in terms of gender, we won't change the needle on the dial of inclusion. Without the needle shifting, we will continue to miss out on a world of potential, and I believe we will be stuck in our current set of problems. The brain that created the problem is rarely where the solution lies.

'Problems cannot be solved with the same mindset that created them.'

Albert Einstein

We need to gain an understanding from those who experience exclusion – what it feels like and the root causes – and then we need those who do not experience this to stand alongside and call out the 'bad' behaviour (with empathy). Allyship is the difference that will make the difference at the point we are currently at in the world with inclusion and acceptance. An ally recognises unearned privileges in their personal lives and in the workplace and acts on inequalities by taking responsibility to end patterns of injustice. From their place of privilege, they can break down barriers, build up support and sponsorship, and enable networks to be built that empower and level the playing field.

For example, according to a report by *Harvard Business Review*, when men are deliberately engaged in gender inclusion programmes, 96% of organisations see progress, compared to only 30% of organisations where men are not engaged. Many organisations still focus their diversity and inclusion efforts on women or, at best, invite men to attend events designed for women. Men can face penalties for supporting women's advancement and for failing to conform to masculine norms, so to create more and better male allies, organisations and women's advocates, I believe we must recognise that allyship can take many forms and varieties. It is not one-size-fits-all, and men who want to be allies can focus on listening, support and respect, no matter what the context.

Read the room – building sensory acuity

To be able to change anything in life and to take an approach to making the change that fits the moment, we need to be masters of noticing what is really going on. In our busy lives, we can all too often be running through parts of our day on autopilot. When autopilot kicks in, we can be blind to realities. Research shows that once our brains are familiar with an activity, they 'switch off' and go into autopilot mode or default mode network (DMN) state, which allows us to undertake tasks without actually thinking about them. Even more strangely, it showed that the brain seemed to perform the tasks better and with more accuracy when in DMN. Consider those activities you do where this most likely is true for you. Things like playing a musical instrument, driving a familiar route or tying your shoelaces. For these types of activities, autopilot can be hugely beneficial, and it often conserves brain power for tasks that may need more focus or creativity. DMN becomes an issue when we want to make a change, though, because we do not really notice what is going on. It would take an out-of-the-ordinary occurrence to knock us back into the full functionality of our brain's sensory acuity. Something like a pedestrian walking out as you drive home would kick you immediately out of your DMN state. The problem here is that often the very processes, structures and behaviours that are holding the patriarchy or exclusive system in place are happening where we are familiar and DMN is in full effect. The equivalent of being kicked out of autopilot by the pedestrian stepping out could be that you only notice the neurodiverse child when they are screaming in the corner and covering their ears, as the rest of the children bang their feet on the floor loudly to the music. Or at work you may not hear the 'banter' that makes those who work flexibly/part-time feel like they are 'slackers' because they aren't in the office every day or at every meeting online. You don't notice the sometimes subtle stages before they resign and take their talents elsewhere. For every woman promoted into a management position, there are two leaving.[3] So what is happening that makes this their only option? What can you affect that could shift things? What aren't you seeing or hearing on a daily basis that is pushing them closer to choosing not to remain? When it comes to gender equity in the workplace, we still have a long way to go, and each of us can make small changes that will have a massive ripple effect to shift this.

Everyday ways to promote equity and inclusion:

- Speak up against insensitive comments. If someone you know makes an insensitive comment about a person's gender, race or sexual orientation, call attention to the comment and explain how it does not promote inclusion.

- Give everyone a voice.

- Learn to listen.

- Think about whose voices are present/not present and invite in the unheard.

Behaviour follows the emotion

Our reactions to others change depending on what we are feeling at any given moment. For example, when we feel sympathy, we show that we feel sorry for the person or animal in question and might donate money to a charity. However, if, in the same circumstance, we feel empathy, we would more likely choose to do something to help alleviate the suffering. With this understanding that how we feel makes a difference to our behaviour, it seems blatantly clear to me as to why we must come from a place of empathy when calling out bad behaviour to be able to model embracing difference and go on to change the world. When it comes to inequity, it is not enough to acknowledge the issue and sympathise with a 'poor them'; we need to lean in and proactively level the playing field. It is no longer enough to accept that things just are the way they are. When thinking about gender equity as an example, if we continue to sympathise rather than truly empathise and act, then, according to a report published by UN Women in September 2022,[4] it could take close to 300 years to achieve full gender equality at the current rate of progress. Not good enough! You will find similarly shocking stats, no matter which minority group you might choose to look at. Within our sphere of influence and control, we all have to find ways to create equity in the now so that it becomes the new normal for future generations.

I came across a great example of this recently when I was visiting a large car dealership that I work with as a coach. Over the last few years, they have been investing in training and education around diversity, equity and inclusion for all team members. As I went out to the workshop to say hi to the technicians and apprentices, I was walking through the parts storage area and office, and I noticed a new desk area had been created off the side, away from the noise of the technicians' bays and that soundproof partitions had been put in place. I got curious and asked the parts team manager what was happening. As soon as they started to tell me about Abu, the new parts apprentice, I felt the pride and saw the huge smile on the faces of the general manager and the parts team. During interviews, they had received a letter from a young man who had applied for over 30 roles since leaving college. He has both a physical disability, which means he uses sticks to be stable when he walks, and a sensory processing disorder, which means that loud noises cause him to become overwhelmed in an instant. The managers at the site could see that he had the most positive attitude and a real thirst to want to work, so they took the steps to work with him to create a working space that could meet his needs. They set up a three-month 'suck it and see' period so the young man and the team could figure out if this was a good place for him to bring his talents. Being open to making reasonable changes to the environment and having open dialogue with the person who had previously been written off or excluded has made a massive difference. The difference that the whole team feel across the site now they have such a cheerful and upbeat (as well as forcefully resilient) new apprentice onboard is palpable.

Stepping into their shoes first

A great question to ask yourself as a new daily habit is, 'What else might be true here?' We can so often get stuck in our 'truths' and act as if they are the only option. This may be because we have not stopped to pause and think about what else may work. As humans, we jump from thought to action rather quickly, and most systems are set up to reward this as a behaviour. It can take us down the wrong path, create an obvious short-term unintended impact, or even set us up for a longer-term and more 'in the ether'-type unintended consequence. It's how the unwritten rules come into being. We've all worked in places or visited with others where it's taken a while to figure out the answer to the question, 'How should we act around here?' We map across what is acceptable from one place to another without consciously thinking about it. I remember the first realisation I had of this in the workplace was back in my mid-twenties when I'd been working in banking for a while and then moved to a national DIY chain (part of my wiggly career path, but that's a different story). In the bank, when you were on a break, you could go to the staff room and make yourself a cuppa using the tea bags and milk that were provided. So during my first week on-site at the DIY store, I was just finishing with my official induction training when there was a break. As we had 15 minutes before the next thing was happening, I took myself off to the staff room to have a cup of tea. I went about doing similar for the rest of the week until, on the Friday, Pat, a friendly older colleague, took pity on me and took me to one side. I'd been causing real gossip and anger amongst the team, and they thought I was really 'stuck up'. This confused me as no one had said anything to me, and on the surface everyone was friendly. Pat shared that, at the store, everything in the fridge belonged to someone and that all week I'd been stealing milk and tea bags from teammates. I was devastated and went to apologise immediately, and the lesson about assumptions and unwritten rules has stuck with me ever since. Here, I was simply mapping across what was 'normal' in my first job, and it had minor consequences because someone had the courage to proactively step in and put me on track. If Pat hadn't done that, then I would have become truly isolated and unable to do my job, and I would probably have ended up leaving because you cannot get your job done in isolation – you need your team. All this would have happened without knowing why the problem had occurred or why I was being shunned. This story may be about something as innocuous as a cup of tea, but imagine if there are things that make it impossible for you to access what you need to do your job or to live. You simply don't know about them because no one has had the courage to tell you. If the team had stepped into my shoes and asked themselves, 'What else might be true here?', rather than assuming I was too privileged and snooty to buy my own tea, they would have solved the issue immediately. A simple 'Sarah, we have to provide our own refreshments here' would have stopped the issue from ever occurring.

How often do you check in with yourself and notice the unwritten rules that are playing out within your family, team or organisation? Who are you excluding as a result of the way things 'just are'? Let's all take a moment and pause, step back, and really have a look at the norms we run. Are they enabling others to step into their full potential, or are they, at best, just allowing those already in situ to keep doing what they've always done?

Tip

Question, question, question, pause and then act.

Be clear about your expectations.

Make the unwritten 'rules' explicit.

In everyday life, this plays out regularly, and the ripple effect across families and therefore communities is huge, even if it is going unnoticed by many. Think about the last time you were in a supermarket and saw a child 'playing up'. How did you and others respond? When you next see that child having a meltdown in the market or running around in an area that isn't ideal, like a train or café, stop yourself from jumping straight to your usual narrative. I've been on the receiving end of the shaming looks, blatant tuts and unhelpful comments about how I should be parenting my son and telling him to sit still or that he must not x/y/z. With his autism, ADHD and attachment challenges, he needs to move; it's as simple as that. When he starts to become dysregulated or wobbly, he may make noises to calm himself, and he can tip over into what looks like a tantrum, but in reality is his brain shutting down and his body doing all it can to make whatever is happening stop. You can never know what is behind the behaviour you are observing, so please be kind first.

Story

A few years ago, I was working with a team in the north of England who ran a large technical services division. They had around eight customer-facing advisers at the site I was visiting, along with around five back-office staff, and throughout the day you were likely to see most of the ten field-based engineering team as they drove in to pick up the next job. I spent time with the front-of-house advisers to observe how they interacted and to help me understand more of their world before I met with the management team to build some team coaching objectives later that day. As I sat watching from just inside a nearby office, I heard a couple of the back-office team complaining about George. George had just come in from the field to collect a job, snapped at an adviser and left them in quite an emotional state. The manager intended to speak with him when he came back on-site to make him apologise and to reprimand him for the behaviour. Listening to the back-office team, I heard that one of them knew George's wife and that he had recently been going to the hospital for tests, and they were waiting to hear if his cancer had returned. The results were due that day and must have been making him feel really anxious, distracted and certainly not his best self. Having heard this, I pulled the manager aside to share, without breaking any confidences about the details, that there was more to the behaviour than he may have realised and that instead of an apology-seeking and reprimand-giving conversation, he might be better to call George in, go for a walk or a cup of tea and find out how he was. George's behaviour was out of the ordinary for him, and the first reaction of the team needed to be to step into his shoes, empathise, and find out what was going on for him. Seeking to understand first and then react based on the full picture led to a much better outcome for the whole team and, ultimately, the customers.

All behaviour is a form of communication, so when something happens that is unexpected or that has a negative impact, we need to first explore what's going on. Take a breath, get curious, consider the options and then act.

Dualisms

In psychological terms, dualistic thinking is a type of reasoning where people perceive only two distinct and opposing options. This type of thinking is versus thinking, where we have a tendency to map different concepts into mutually opposite categories. It is binary in its nature and limits our thinking. While dualisms can help us to make meaning and navigate life, it is a habit that will always limit options and can often lead to exclusion. For example, people who see the 'nature versus nurture' issue as a binary rather than a spectrum context are falling victim to dualistic thinking. For us to develop our societies and organisations and become more inclusive, we have to see the spectrum – not simply two options. Sitting with the discomfort of not knowing the full and final right answer is key. If we hold dualisms lightly as something that may be useful as a frame but not the truth, we will build our tolerance of difference and ambiguity.

Dualistic thinking examples:

- Nature versus Nurture

- Male versus Female

- Healthy versus Unhealthy

- Good versus Evil

- Capitalism versus Communism

- Rich versus Poor

- Faith versus Logic

- Right versus Wrong

- Individuality versus Collectivism

- Liberalism versus Conservatism

Exercise: Dualism busting

Notice which dualisms you may hold from the list above. What others could you add to the list? What else may also be true?

Once you have your own list of the ones that resonate for you, get some A4 paper. On each sheet, write one half of the dualism (e.g., one sheet for Good and one for Evil), then place them on the floor around two metres apart. Stand in between the two sheets and notice what else belongs or could fit on the floor if you were to create a spectrum between the two. Stand on the page with Evil on it and ask yourself, 'What is one step closer to Good?' Once you have completed the spectrum, step back and notice how much more choice this gives you.

Life is more spectrum than binary. Learning to articulate the spectrum on things we hold dualisms in place for can be liberating.

Making others wrong

No one has ever changed their behaviour in a sustainable way by being told that they are wrong. If we are told that what we are doing – the task – is wrong, then we may take it on and adapt, but if we are made to feel wrong as a person, then our fight, flight, freeze (or flop) reaction kicks in.

As human beings, we are programmed for survival, so when our amygdala gets pricked in our brain, we react in a way that keeps us alive. Our brains don't differentiate between whether it is a physical or psychological threat. Where there is no physical threat, this is commonly known as an amygdala hijack. We respond in a way that is out of kilter with the stimuli. In these situations or ones where it is likely you may cause an amygdala hijack by raising a topic, we need to take a dose of our own advice when we choose to call out bad behaviour. We must begin by stepping into the other person's shoes. What might be going on for them that is making them behave a particular way? How might you best name the issue without it being taken at an identity level? It doesn't mean that you accept the behaviour; it means that you will approach the subject with empathy and in a way that can be heard and, more importantly, give the opportunity for them to respond with the executive functioning part of the brain still online.

The language really matters with this. For example, if a member of your team sends you a piece of work that is not as you expected, you could easily make them feel wrong as a person by saying, 'You've not done a good enough job with this report. You need to include more detail.' An alternate way of feeding back that changes are needed that doesn't make the person feel wrong while clearly saying what is needed could be, 'This report needs more detail to hit the brief. When do you think you can get onto it?'

Forgiveness doesn't work

Many people consider forgiveness something that is expected of them and is necessary to be able to move on from something that was painful or difficult. Often, these beliefs are embedded in the culture we grow up in or our religion. The problem is that this sense of duty can often lead to resentment and unprocessed feelings.

In my early years, I was an empathetic child and young person who often would take on the responsibility for other people's feelings. This sense of needing to make everyone feel okay is something I carried well into my thirties until I was lucky enough to encounter the practice of coaching constellations, a modality that comes from the work of Bert Hellinger, a therapist and psychoanalyst. It encourages taking full responsibility for our own actions, choices, thoughts and feelings. Although we are responsible for ourselves and those in our care who are vulnerable, such as children, elderly dependants or the disabled, we are not responsible for friends, colleagues or lovers. These people are our equals.

The family constellation philosophy is driven by a concept of things having a natural order. This means that each person in the system, be it family, friendship or organisation, has a rightful place. Whoever came first in the system came first. So for instance, if you are the youngest child, then you are smaller than your elder siblings and parents, even when you are all grown up. They have seen more sunrises and sunsets. The philosophy requires us to have the maturity to reflect on our part in situations, to take full responsibility for ourselves and then both mentally and emotionally leave the rest with the other. If we get into the space of forgiveness, we are taking the opportunity to be adult away from the other person, and we are making ourselves bigger than they are. We could even be considered to be placing ourselves as 'saint-like' when, in reality, we are not better than them. Fundamentally, we are equal human beings.

So instead of 'forgiving' others, we need to accept reality as it is, acknowledge the pain and honour the experience. For things to change at a systemic level, we must find a way to call out the behaviour from a place of equality and being the same size. This way, while feeling the discomfort, things can be acknowledged as the way they are, and we can let it go and move on to what is next. If we demonise the current behaviours or the past, then we are feeding energy into the system in a way that keeps things stuck.

Tips on healthily letting go

1. Be intentional – take the time to process your thoughts and emotions.

2. Notice resistance – pay attention to any resistance you feel to letting go, notice any patterns and sit with the discomfort until it moves on and through you.

3. Set some expectations around how much time you might want or need to feel the pain or discomfort.

4. Honour your emotions AND stop blaming others.

5. Focus on what you can control.

All behaviour is communication

One of the greatest gifts we have as human beings is the art of communication. Everyone communicates through behaviour, even when they aren't using words. A baby may cry to let the caregiver know they are wet, hungry or tired, just as adults may yawn as a sign of boredom. Adults and children are communicating every moment of every day, even if they are unaware of it. All challenging behaviour meets a need for the individual. Behaviour that is labelled as challenging is often expressing an unmet need. This reframing of the behaviour can help you with not taking the actions personally. It gives you a place to go that is more solution-focused and asks the question, 'What is this behaviour telling me?' It's important for us to understand more about behaviour as a form of communication to be able to make better decisions about our response.

Attachment and early years trauma

In most families, babies learn how to have their needs met through a cycle of positive attachment. A baby cries, and a caregiver will respond, figure out what the baby needs and then meet the need. At a visceral level, this leads to the baby learning that the world is a safe place and that their needs will be met. They develop secure attachment. In many families, this cycle may have been interrupted, and the baby cries, the caregiver doesn't respond, and the needs are either not met at all or they are inconsistently met.

Research indicates that 55% of the population display a secure attachment pattern. Children who have an avoidant attachment pattern have learnt that their emotions are not responded to empathically. Such children have learnt to anticipate that expressions of their emotions will anger or irritate their carer. These beliefs and behaviours continue into adulthood for many. With 45% of the population outside of the secure attachment reality, we are likely to be working and living with many whose behaviours need first to be understood rather than reacted to.

To be able to embrace difference, we need to be in a position where we have looked inward and done our own exploration and healing. If we have a background of insecure attachment, then we may find ourselves triggered by, or even creating, situations that are chaotic. Comfort can be found in the familiar, even when it is seemingly difficult. Change will only happen when the pain of staying the same is greater than the pain of change or if there is so much pleasure in the new that it draws you out of the current situation.

Exercise: Discover your attachment style

The first step here is understanding your own attachment style and recognising it without judgement. This will help you to understand others' responses to you and choose your reaction rather than be automatically triggered.

Read the descriptions of the four adult attachment styles listed below and notice which seems to resonate with you most. Once you've identified which you believe is the best fit for you, spend time over the next few weeks testing and observing your own behaviours to calibrate. Check in with those who know you well and check back in with your own views to get to your own most accurate self-assessment. Understanding our own style can open us up to a deeper understanding of our own and others' behaviours, giving us more choice and flexibility.

Here are the four main attachment styles:

- **Secure attachment** refers to those who have the ability to form secure, loving relationships – to be able to trust, love and become close to others with relative ease. They are comfortable with intimacy and do not panic or become anxious when their partners need space or time away from them.

'I find it pretty easy to get close to others and feel comfortable depending on them and having them depend on me in return. I don't often worry about someone getting too close to me or abandoning me.'

- **Anxious/Preoccupied attachment** is one of the three insecure attachment styles and is marked by a deep fear of abandonment. People with this style are often worried that their partner will leave them, and they hungrily seek validation. It can be associated with being 'clingy' or 'needy', such as when a partner or friend doesn't text you back fast enough so are considered to not care enough.

'Others don't seem to want to get as close as I would like. I want to merge completely with the other person, and this can often scare people away. I often find myself worrying that my partner doesn't really want to stay with me or that they love me.'

- **Avoidant/Dismissive attachment** is the next insecure attachment style and is the one where intimacy is feared. Getting close to people and trusting feel unsafe because ultimately the person doesn't feel their needs can be met in a relationship. In relationships, avoidant people typically maintain a distance and can be experienced by others as emotionally unavailable. They may even avoid relationships altogether as they find them suffocating.

'Being close to others makes me uncomfortable and I find it difficult to trust them completely or let myself depend on them. When anyone gets close, it makes me nervous, and often partners want me to be more open and intimate than I feel able to be.'

- **Fearful/Avoidant attachment** is the third and most complex of the insecure attachment styles as it is a combination of both the anxious and avoidant types. People with this style are reluctant to develop close romantic relationships, yet at the same time they feel a deep need to feel loved by others. They desperately crave affection and want to avoid it at all costs. This style is often termed the disorganised attachment style as it is inconsistent in its presentation of behaviours. It is thought to be the rarest of the styles.

"I don't feel worthy of love and affection and I have difficulty trusting others. I often have internal conflicts where I want to feel loved and yet I am too afraid of getting hurt by loved ones, so usually I avoid getting close to them or relying on them in any way. I may let them get close but then I push them away."

To explore further, go to the attachment project website and take their five-minute attachment-style quiz: https://www.attachmentproject. com/attachment-style-quiz/

Labels matter

When I'm talking about labels here, I am referring to the labels you call yourself in your head. They are tags that you attach to yourself to describe the person you think you are. Are you a successful career woman, a super mum, a loser, an ugly person, a go-getter, a 'fatty', a good-for-nothing? We put ourselves in boxes to define who we are.

These labels are ones that are given to us at an early age, often by people who are in positions of authority, and they can impact our sense of who we are. They become the truth for us internally in terms of our identity. Words are powerful, and we like to be right, so often we will choose a path to living up to the labels we are given. If you were called 'the class clown', 'the tomboy' or 'the bookworm', then chances are you owned the behaviours that matched the name. This may not have happened at first calling, but where repetitive labelling occurs, it is most likely that we choose the path of least resistance. What happens around the person with the label is that others filter their experiences of the individual through the lens of the name. So if you are expecting Naughty Nick to show up, then your confirmation bias will kick in, and you will notice behaviours you might consider normal in others as naughty for him. You anticipate and so call up certain behaviours and then respond accordingly in interactions, and in so doing, make yourself correct. We've all had instances where we've misjudged someone based on others' opinions or first impressions. Noticing the labels you own or that you hand out to others is an important step in creating inclusive environments.

Labels can be used to positive effect as they reflect how a person feels about themselves or others. They not only influence how a personal identity is created but also allow for recognition that others have different qualities. They aid people in understanding differences in needs, culture and personalities.

Stereotyping can be behind many of the labels that are given and may lead to prejudicial behaviours. An example would be that all young men wearing hoodies are hoodlums, so when you see them you cross the street. Not all gender stereotypes on their own are right or wrong. People have a choice as to whether they conform to the culture-based norm. It's when we judge others because they don't adhere to the traditional gender stereotype that problems arise. If you are a woman and want to become the CEO of a major organisation or work in STEM, you won't get far by believing the gender stereotypes in the media that often portray men as being in charge. If you're a man who wants to be a midwife or nurse, you may also encounter discrimination and judgement because stereotypes dictate you should become a doctor and stay out of the delivery room. With these types of outdated attitudes, so many organisations are depriving society of workers who would thrive in non-traditional jobs and contribute to society in a really positive way.

Ways to help break the stereotyping:

1. Read books and watch films in which the main character is a woman and she's not the love interest. Start children young with books like *Zog and the Flying Doctors*.

2. Actively seek out and acknowledge contributions to history from all genders and races.

3. Participate equally in household chores and childcare.

4. Learn skills based on what interests you and encourage young women to excel in STEM subjects.

5. Emphasise accomplishments over physical attributes.

6. Choose colours based on personal preference.

Brain filtering and neurodivergence

Our judgements of ourselves, others and the way we make sense of the world can only ever be a filtered version. Remember earlier when we explored the way the neurotypical brain filters based on prefaces, generalisations, distortions and the like to be able to avoid overwhelm? Well imagine now if you are neurodivergent and find yourself judged against standards and 'rules' that aren't even designed for your brain. It's the classic 'don't judge a fish by its ability to climb a tree' situation. With 15–20% of the population being neurodivergent, it is a huge loss to society and businesses to not embrace the differences. Raising our awareness of the difference and what adjustments can easily and reasonably be made so that every kind of mind can contribute feels like an obvious thing to do to me. Whether it is autism, ADHD, dyslexia or some other difference we are speaking about, the aim has to be to enable more people to fulfil their long-term potential.

The diversity of thought that including neurodiversity brings is critical to an innovative workforce. In my opinion, it is where sustainable success in business lies. The world is constantly changing, and we need to be able to flex and adapt. From a societal perspective, it is not just morally the right thing to do, but it also makes financial sense. For example, only 16% of autistic adults are in full-time paid employment, according to the National Autistic Society. If organisations were open to adapting working environments and cultural aspects that enable inclusion, the amount saved on funding support for the 84% who could be working would pay for the reasonable adjustments needed a thousandfold. This makes financial sense as much as it is an ethical no-brainer.

When faced with behaviours that don't seem to fit your expectations, it is worth considering what may be the cause of the mismatch. Could it be that your expectations were based on a neurotypical world? At a recent client meeting where the team were discussing recruitment for a new technical role, I noticed some expectations that were being stated that would potentially exclude those with autism/ADHD. The job description included 'excellent communication skills' and 'good team player' when they were not essential for the job to be carried out effectively. For many people with autism or ADHD, social norms and niceties aren't part of their way of being. So seeing these often-default skills included would lead them to believe they are ineligible for the role and so wouldn't apply. Understanding at interviews that holding eye contact or handling conceptual 'what if' style conversations are simply not accessible to many neurodiverse individuals and may cause a meltdown or overwhelm is key to levelling the playing field when it comes to the job market.

CHAPTER 4

Honour the past to change the future

Looking to the future is a really positive trait and one that creates momentum and change. Without acknowledging the past, though, you could be dragging along all sorts of baggage or unhelpful followers that don't serve your goals for the future. Without all that has happened to date, we would not be in the place we are today. Delusion is thinking that we can have a blank sheet and begin from today as if yesterday didn't exist.

Knowing where we've come from means we can notice positive change and do more

On any journey, you need to know both your current location and your future destination. Milestone markers along the way are helpful, too, as you can check in that you are not only on track but going in the right direction. When it comes to changing cultural norms and what is acceptable, the markers of success are really nuanced in the first instance. To begin measuring how many times banter is unacceptable or what percentage of the comments you hear that could be considered a slur to a minority is a very blunt marker. In my opinion, we need to hear these and have zero tolerance. Calling things out with empathy in the way described in the previous chapter is an art – one that needs to be practised by all and, because we are all human, is rarely perfected. But it's important to have a feel for the current status of things in your environment, even though empirically measuring things may be counterproductive.

Pace, pace, pace, then lead

Here, I am making the assumption that in our communications, we want to have an influence on others. If that influence is to reinforce the current status, the communication has purpose rather than just being a noise to fill the silence. In order to have influence, you must first pace the person's or group's model of reality. This doesn't mean agreeing with them, but it does mean holding your opinions, listening and being open to actually hearing their view. Being able to step into another person's reality to wonder what would need to be true for them to have this perception is a really powerful and useful skill, and it's essential to communicate effectively in a way that has influence. Once you have paced them in their reality, you can then lead them to where you want them to go much more effectively.

In general, our culture is much more aligned with fixing things – with problem-solving. This approach can be effective when you are dealing with mechanics or objects. When it comes to creating an inclusive culture, people are involved. Old habits need to change, and new norms need to be set. If you're aiming to create a space where all are able to be themselves and flourish without fear or loss, then this problem-solving approach will not work. Acknowledging how addicted we are to fixing things and an action orientation may be one of the first steps to systemic change. We need to allow ourselves to model excellence, to find the places where we are already being inclusive and discover the fine detail in their 'how'. The fine detail is where the keys are, and the power of the change is in adapting to make things transferable into your context. This depends on where you are today. A cultural example I remember from my past was back when the large DIY organisation I worked for was looking to expand into the Far East. They cleverly learned from the mistakes of a British supermarket chain who had the year before attempted to lift their business model and operational processes into the Chinese culture... and failed. The team in charge of the China project at my organisation first set out to find local examples of excellence and then took our existing successful ways of working and created a beautiful new version. They learned from the modelling exercise that people in Shanghai weren't in a space where DIY would work. They moved into properties where finished meant that the wires were still coming out of the wall, so you needed to have tradespeople involved when it came to decorating and finishing property. The new Eastern version was BIY (buy it yourself). They paced the new customers to meet them in their current culture and then took them one step towards DIY by leading them to BIY. For us to do the same in terms of equity in the workplace, we need to locate those examples where things have changed.

Company examples:

- Sodexo have found that their focus on gender equity and creating an optimal balance within the organisation have led to employee engagement scores increasing (4%), gross profit increasing (23%) and brand image strengthening (5%). Their focus doesn't end with gender, though, as they also have more than 18 LGBTQ+ and ally employee networks around the world. They are modelling themselves and mapping what works across different groups where greater inclusion is required and desirable.

- Mastercard is consistently named in the top ten global lists for diversity and inclusion awards. They work hard to ensure equal pay, and 81% of final candidate interviews include women, so they are definitely doing something right with their recruitment policies and pay and reward practices. They also offer expansive practical employee benefits that go beyond maternity/paternity/adoption leave, like coverage for sex reassignment surgery and surrogacy assistance.

These are two of a cluster of companies that are doing a lot to embrace diversity and inclusion in a big way. Others include Johnson & Johnson, Accenture, EY, Cisco, Marriott International and Novartis. In the tech space, Microsoft, LinkedIn and Netflix are also front-runners. With more than half of Fortune 500 companies now having a chief diversity officer, the benefits of making this change are being seen and acted upon more readily. Sadly, the World Economic Forum recently predicted that it would take 135.6 years to close the gender gap worldwide based on the current rate of progress. Not good enough!

Country examples:

Nordic countries top most of the diversity lists, thanks to their gender-equitable labour policies, healthcare access, and representation in both government and leadership positions. For things to change in a sustainable way, we need to look beyond the organisational impact and consider how society is impacted by the way countries are governed and the choices that need to be made to live. Think about it for a moment – if half the population of a country are hampered by restricted opportunities, then economic targets and sustainable development goals are simply unachievable.

The World Economic Forum compiles and releases the Global Gender Gap Index (GGGI) every year. This report measures and shows the extent of gender-based gaps amongst four key dimensions: economic participation and opportunity; educational attainment; health and survival; and political empowerment. Below are the GGGI rankings for 2023, with Iceland retaining its number-one spot for the 12th year.

Country	GGGI 2023
Iceland	0.91
Norway	0.88
Finland	0.86
New Zealand	0.86
Germany	0.81
Sweden	0.81
Nicaragua	0.81
Namibia	0.80
Lithuania	0.80
Belgium	0.80

Ranking scores are between 0.00 (the lowest possible gender equality) and 1.00 (100%, the highest possible gender equality).

NB: within the scoring, the largest current gender gap appears in the Political Empowerment category (widening by 2.4%). This is a real concern when you consider that 81 countries have never had a female head of state.

Future pacing is a brilliant technique that helps you to get a sense of something more fully and to clarify and tune into the world you want to create. It enables you to test ahead of time how you will be in a future situation. As you play out the future scenario, you notice the effects on your intentions, and you get to clarify what it will take for you to be at your best. It enables you to mentally rehearse so that you are better equipped and more likely to achieve the outcomes you desire when the time comes. It allows you to notice what's missing or not as you want it and then to recalibrate your planned actions and behaviours accordingly.

Exercise: How to future pace

1. Take a moment to go inside and think about the part of your world that you wish to influence and change in service of embracing difference to change the world. Imagine how you want it to be in the future. Be as specific as you can. Perhaps think of a specific situation that is coming up where you want to be at your best in service of creating equity and inclusion.

2. As you create the image, stay disassociated, i.e., see yourself in the situation in the future as if you are watching a movie. Run the movie and observe what happens. You may want to run several versions of the movie to find different ways to achieve your outcome.

3. Check your response to what happens as a result of YOUR behaviour. Does it feel congruent and aligned, or is part of you resisting or objecting?

4. Make adjustments to the movie as necessary. Tweak what you have, or begin again even.

5. Run the movie again with the changes and notice what happens this time.

6. Once it feels aligned and congruent, allow yourself to 'step into the movie' in your imagination and live the experience.

7. When you are satisfied with the result, exit the mental rehearsal.

8. Now let go. Your conscious mind has played its part, and now it's time to trust your other-than-conscious mind to run with the message.

Landmark dates for women

1867

1867 National Society for Women's Suffrage is formed; Lydia Becker becomes secretary of the Manchester Society

1870 Married Women's Property Act comes into effect, allowing married women to own property

1903 Emmeline Pankhurst founds the VVomen's Social and Political Union (WSPU), which later becomes known as the suffragettes

1905 Militant campaign begins; Christabel Pankhurst and Annie Kenney are arrested for assault and imprisoned

1907 The Women's Freedom League (WFL) emerges from the WSPU, rejecting the dominance of the Pankhursts

1908 Mass rally in London; between 300,000 and 500,000 activists gather in Hyde Park and windows are smashed in Downing Street

1909 Start of suffragette hunger strikes and force-feeding in prison

1910 On what became known as Black Friday, women protest at Westminster as the Conciliation Bill (which would have given them the vote) fails to pass. 115 women are arrested and two die

1913 Emily Wilding Davison throws herself under the King's horse; the 'Cat and Mouse' Act means hunger strikers are temporarily released from prison so they don't die in police custody

1918 Representation of the People Act grants women over 30 the right to vote (and men over 21 the same right)

1928 Women over 21 are given equal voting rights with men

1929 Margaret Bonclfield becomes the first female cabinet minister

1929

1956 Legal reforms require equal pay for female teachers and civil servants

1961 Contraception (including the Pill) becomes available for married women on the NHS

1967 The Abortion Act decriminalises abortion in Britain on certain grounds

1970 The Equal Pay Act, prohibiting any less favourable treatment between men and women in terms of pay, becomes law

1979 Margaret Thatcher becomes Britain's first female prime minister

1991 Rape within marriage is made a crime

2018 Under equal pay legislation, by 4 April this year employers with more than 250 staff are required to report salary figures for men and women

Pathway to change

History matters, and it is a place to reflect about and learn from, not a place to live. With that in mind, I want us to spend a second or two looking back over some of the moments on the pathway of gender equality and neurodiversity so we can notice where we have come from and then realise the speed we now need to deploy to create meaningful shifts for the next generation.

Some cultures are yet to accept the paradigm of neurodiversity and believe that experiences of ADHD, autism, etc. are all forms of mental health disorders. Behaviours that are classed as different or difficult vary widely because of the different expectations of social behaviours and social norms. In the 1800s in the UK, those displaying symptoms of mental health were locked away from society in mental asylums and very often left to die in squalid and inhumane conditions. Over time, society would use these institutions as places to lock away those who they felt weren't 'like them', including those we would now consider to have low-level learning difficulties or be neurodiverse. The rapid expansion of new institutions in the 19th century, when many people with disabilities were moved from their communities into asylums and workhouses, is shocking. According to the National Autistic Society, as of January 2022 there were 1,185 autistic people held within the inpatient psychiatric system.[5] Of these, around one in seven (165) were under 18 years of age! As the mother of an autistic child, this leaves me breathless.

If these are some of the things that in the past were thought of as normal and now seem barbaric, then what else are we still doing that in another generation or two will also seem inhumane? We need to fast-track our thinking and find ways to shift the behaviours across society. Daily small changes make a difference. Saying no to things that are unacceptable or that are just habits, even if they seem small, will shift things. Finding new ways to proactively step into a new norm and desensitise those around us makes change more possible. An example for me in recent years has been to own and name my perimenopausal story, from sitting in group meetings with a hand fan to cool myself when a flush comes rather than attempting to hide it, to calling a client to explain I'd be there a few minutes after our planned meet time because I'd got the wrong bus due to brain fog. This latter one is a great example of a small shift that started a powerful conversation, so let me elaborate:

Story

This is a story of a trip to a client site where I worked as a coach/consultant for over a decade. I had done the commute to the site from the same start point every time, so I could do it in my sleep – or I could prior to perimenopause and the joy of brain fog moments. I'd leave the flat in Kilburn and walk up to the High Road to get the number 32 bus up to Colindale. Anyone who knows that part of London will be able to tell you that this route is a straight line up the A5. You get on the 32 bus, which is a double-decker, stay on it for around 25–30 minutes, hop off at the stop opposite McDonald's and then walk the final few minutes of the journey to the office. On this day, though, I got on the bus, and around 15 minutes later it turned left. I noticed and thought it odd, so I hopped off at the next stop to figure out what was happening. As I stood in Dollis Hill, a realisation dawned as the single-decker number 332 bus pulled off the stand that I had got on completely the wrong bus – one that had one less deck and one more 3 in its number! At this moment, I had a choice. I could feel ashamed that I had made such a silly mistake and phone the client, blaming traffic or all sorts of other things for the fact that I would be a few minutes later than planned. Or I could take the opportunity to own my reality and normalise the effects of the menopause I was experiencing. After choosing to laugh at myself rather than feel ashamed, I booked an Uber and called the client. On the call, I told the full story to his PA with some humour, and she said not to worry and that she'd let Paul (the general manager of the site) know. When I arrived on-site, he shared that his wife was

---

going through the menopause currently, and we got to talking about the challenges it brings, as well as the insights and positive impact it was having both at home and at work. He shared how his personal experience had informed conversations and policy strategising with HR on how to retain staff at this point in their life. He recognised that his knowledge and experience was also helping him to manage client-facing team members better because he could understand their needs more. By talking about his own lived experience, he was helping to make topics like this no longer taboo. It's a real opportunity to build more resilient businesses. When we include the needs of our team at all stages of life, we build loyalty and trust. Relationships are deepened, psychological safety is built, and high performance ensues.

Often I have seen discomfort on the face of others when mentioning things like the menopause. However, the more I openly reference them, the more I notice it becoming easier and 'normal'. If we can do this with whatever topic is live for us, the door will open for those who may not have the confidence, ability or opportunity to impact what can and can't be spoken of, and we can all make a daily difference.

Accepting the truth of what happened doesn't mean the behaviour is okay

The truth is a thing that many seek and that in most situations doesn't exist in one version. We all have different perspectives, and because of the brain filtering that I've spoken of earlier in this book, we do literally all have different truths (remember the 2 million bits of data per second and the 134 bits the neurotypical brain can manage). Holding our own truths lightly is a practice that can make for a well-lived life and one that has a greater tolerance for change. To be able to include the possibility of something that is not your held belief or 'rule' is the secret sauce when it comes to creating inclusive spaces, groups and communities. Acceptance of the reality of what is enables us to have a greater bandwidth to process what has happened and then react in a way that is both appropriate and useful. To accept an action or situation does not mean that you must be agreeing to it or colluding with the behaviour. If you were mugged or your home was burgled, it would be completely appropriate to be angry and to show it. It is also healthier for you to accept what has happened, to name it, and then allow yourself to process the emotions rather than carry the injustice with you. Putting yourself in the position of choosing your reaction once you have accepted the reality takes courage and practice. Holding your boundary and stating your need or doing what you require in any moment is a really healthy thing to be able to do. It isn't always easy, and there will be times when it may even seem impossible, but it is worth it.

Last summer, we had an instance where we were visiting with some friends in Cornwall. We decided that we would go into the village to play mini golf as our son finds it difficult to be in a room where adults are talking and he isn't active. As we were looking forward to a catch-up, we decided that doing it while trying to hit golf balls through windmills and the like would be more fun. For this to happen, we needed to get as close to the course as possible, as the busy beach area would be a sensory overload for our son, and his phobia of seagulls would mean that being outside wouldn't be an option if we had too far to walk. We are blessed in that we have a Blue Badge for him due to the severity of need, as without it we wouldn't be able to access many things. Having the space close to the door really matters for us. Because his disability is not visible, we often face prejudice, and this is one instance where this happened. We parked on double yellow lines by the entrance road for the golf, I made sure there was space for the local bus to get through, and then we all went to get out. As we walked past the small café with outside seating next to the golf entrance, an older couple were audibly saying to each other how disgusting it was that people were so selfish and lazy and that they were setting such a bad example for their child. They followed this up with much tutting and huffing. In this moment, I had a choice. I could go back and explain, or I could continue on my way. In this instance, I chose the latter because I knew that if I were to stop, the conversation that ensued wouldn't likely be over in a minute, and my son would then most likely not have the capacity to continue on to the golf. For me to be able to continue and be the upbeat mum, I needed to be in that moment. I had to accept that they were speaking from their map of the world and accept that their perspective and judgement were valid, even if they were incorrect. To accept that what had happened was an expression of their truth and not 'the truth' meant I could leave that with them and continue on my way so that our son could have the fun that we had promised. By acting with agency and taking control of your situation by choosing a response that meets the needs of the moment, you are demonstrating strength, and although you may not always actively be showing the perpetrator that what they are doing/saying will not be tolerated, you are not fuelling the situation in a way that means the very person who needs the support misses out.

Consider the act of acceptance as recognising the reality of the situation without attempting to protest it or change it, while condoning is allowing behaviour that is morally wrong or offensive to continue despite its ramifications. Ramifications and consequences need to be part of your decision-making around when to step in and when to practise silence. In my story above, if the people in the café had been within the earshot of my son, I would have stepped in so that he could know that what we were doing was okay and within the rules. His autistic brain would have needed that reassurance to be able to continue on. As it happened, he did not hear, and his needs were better met by my decision to ignore and be with him rather than lean into my temptation to correct and educate.

Culture affects change

How we behave is affected by how we experience the world. Much of how we experience the world is through a lens of what came before. We learn from our elders, sometimes consciously and definitely unconsciously. Having grown up in the 70s and 80s in West Cornwall, I am very aware that the cultural impacts of the day differed from other parts of the UK, let alone the world. The revolution of the 1960s that rippled through our big cities had definitely not made it to Camborne! With no dual carriageway to connect us to 'up country' and more broad views, and, for me, a strong

Methodist underpinning that clearly, if quietly, told you that marriage followed by child rearing was what was expected for decent young women, you knew very clearly what life choices you needed to make and what your place in the world was. This may explain why, as a 17-year-old, I chose to drop out of school because I had fallen in love. I had been a girl who had pushed against the norms by playing football for the school and by taking mechanics courses rather than more traditional 'feminine' classes, and I was a straight-A student who was headed to be the first in the family to go to university. The pull of the cultural messages of what a good girl does and what a young woman should aim for was unconsciously running the show, though. So instead of following my academic path and continuing to lean into difference, I got a job in a bank, got engaged and started what I considered to be the next logical step in life. (My inner rebel and knowing that this path wasn't mine won out. By 19 I had changed path, and by 24 life was wholly different, but that's another story.) The gift for me in reflecting back on this behaviour at such an early age is that even women who, as girls, were pushing against the system can find themselves conforming. Even those of us who are actively working to make a difference in the space of equality and equity have undercurrents and depths of habit that need surfacing and working with so we don't derail. Societal norms and cultural expectations hold a strong field of control, and unless we become more conscious of it and use our own adult agency to push against it, then nothing will change. So I encourage us all, whatever our gender, background or situation, to take time to notice those moments where, if you were to allow yourself to slow down, you may have alternative choices that you could make – ones that may seem unfamiliar or feel 'off'. Next time you do this, allow yourself to ask the question: whose story are you running? Are societal or cultural norms at play, or is it truly what you want?

According to research, just 16.5% of engineers in the UK are women, and while women make up over half (52%) of lawyers in law firms (men make up 47%), the underrepresentation of women becomes more apparent at senior levels. While 61% of solicitors are female, only 35% are partners. Recent statistics used by the ONS for the business support profession have placed the gender split as high as 94% female to 6% male for the UK!

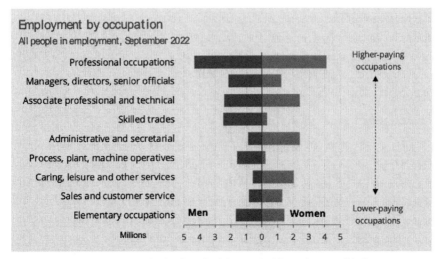

Employment by occupation
All people in employment, September 2022

Note: Occupations ranked based on median hourly pay (excluding overtime) for employees as of April 2022.
Source: ONS, Employment by status and occupation via Nomis and Annual Survey of Hours and Earnings via Nomis

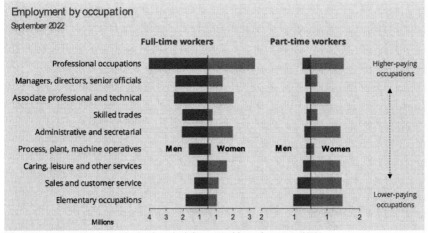

Employment by occupation
September 2022

Note: Occupations ranked based on median hourly pay (excluding overtime) for employees in April 2021.
Source: ONS, Employment by status and occupation and Annual Survey of Hours and Earnings via Nomis.

Without what came before, we wouldn't exist

This is true at the level of the individual, an organisation and society at large. Each person has an origin story and ancestry. Each organisational setting has a history and setup narrative. Family and organisational structures alike have become blended over time. Consider step-parents, adoptions and divorces in the family settings, or takeovers, company purpose and product changes to match society's needs as they shift. Without the caveman, we wouldn't have the wheel; without the wheel, vehicles wouldn't have been possible; without Henry Ford and the use of the moving assembly line, the motor car wouldn't have made it to the masses. The seemingly endless connections and happenings need to be acknowledged and honoured as having gone before because without them we wouldn't be where we are today. The sense of honouring may seem strange when you think about the negative ripples that affect, and indeed in many ways created, the gender inequalities of today. It is important to honour the past, even when it is abhorrent, because the past allows the people of the present and the future to learn without having to endure. We can see how others coped, how they failed, how they survived hard times and how they navigated life. We do not live in the past; we simply accept it for what it is, learn from it and move on. Personal experience is not the only way to learn.

The truth of biology and acceptance

Whatever the current lived experiences and realities of gender fluidity, the biological fact remains that for a human life to begin, you need sperm and an egg. This truth is easy to understand in one way, but the specifics surrounding conception and birth can also be rather complex. Without a biological mother and a biological father, none of us would exist. In organisational settings, the 'birth' of the company will also have an origin. The founder may, of course, be of any gender, and whatever that may be, it is true that they do come first. As time passes, even without acquisitions and mergers taking place, the founder will eventually no longer be present. Be it a sale, handing over the reins to younger generations of the founding family, or death, a time will come when an honouring of the past and stepping into the future is required. Without the founder, the organisation wouldn't exist, but holding on to the founder beyond where they are useful leads to poor health, both for the people and commercially.

The current state of the organisation, family or community is not static. The past does not predict the future – it is no more than something to learn from, to accept as it is, and you need to forge a path forward towards your chosen destination. The key here is acceptance. Without accepting what has been, your energy and attention will always, in part, be stuck in the past. We must learn to take out the hook, let go of the energetic charge and allow ourselves to sit with any discomfort or anger about what has been before. To be able to do this means you can then truly step into a new future, taking the parts that serve your purpose and leaving the rest.

Exercise: Letting go

There are many different techniques for letting go, and you might find some of them a little conceptual. When things are bothering us, there's an energetic charge in both the body and the mind, so I find that doing something that engages both of them is most helpful. Below are the steps to a way of letting go that I've used many a time and that have served my clients well over the years. In extreme cases where tension has been held in the body for a while, I add in an extra step, which is detailed at the bottom.

You will need:

A quiet space, a pen/pencil, a scrap of paper (not a journal), a match/lighter, a safe place to burn paper, a timer and around 15 minutes of time.

Method:

1. Set your timer for 15 minutes, making sure you won't be disturbed (switch your phone off).

2. Start writing by answering the question, 'What is bothering me?'

3. Breathe, and sit with the emotions and bodily sensations that emerge as you think about what is bothering you.

4. Write non-stop and clear out everything that is swirling around in your head and body. Don't worry about the grammar, and allow yourself to swear if that comes up – you don't even need complete sentences. Draw pictures if it's easier, and most of all do not censor yourself. Whatever comes, write it down.

5. Push yourself to write more than you are comfortable with.

6. When you are done, allow yourself to reread what you have written and let the emotions you've been holding come to the surface.

7. Breathe deeply, then burn the paper in a safe place as a symbolic release. You may want to add a verbal affirmation such as, 'The past is over. Today is a new day.'

8. Take some time to relax, walk, take a bath and fill your mind and heart with thoughts and feelings that uplift you.

The additional step I mentioned:

Between steps 6 and 7, if you feel you are holding a lot of tension and stress in your body, then find yourself a stack of cushions and a bat – preferably one of those children's lightweight baseball/ rounders ones. As you stack the cushions, imagine that the situation/ person that is bothering you is on them. Take a deep breath, and while letting out whatever shout or noise that feels right for you, start whacking the cushions. Keep going until your muscles release, and then go back to step 7 above.

This letting-go exercise really works for releasing stresses and worries. Be patient – for most there is a sense of instant release, while for others it can take 24 hours to settle in. You may even find you want to repeat the practice as you process the deeper emotions.

Patterns remain until healing happens – everything has its place

Let's talk epigenetics and the impact of previous generations. I'll begin by stating that I am not a scientist. Psychology and the neuroscience of behavioural change are my areas of expertise, and the world that is science has been known in my youth to bring me to tears – I remember sitting at the back of the room in that A Level physics class feeling so confused I cried! So what I share here is through a layperson's lens and comes from the time I have been blessed being able to spend with some incredibly clever and studious people. The understanding of the magic of working with generational trauma and epigenetics also comes from personal therapeutic experience, so it has been verified in my own life experience.

When we consider how we begin to get to a level of embracing difference that will bring all the changes we need in this world, we need to be ready for the change. I believe the act of getting ready requires us to understand generational impacts on stereotypes and therefore how inclusive or judgemental we may be.

When trauma occurs, and there have been many when you look through the history of feminism and the neurodivergent, chemical marks are made on a person's genes that can be passed down to future generations. This mark doesn't cause a genetic mutation, but it does alter the mechanism by which the gene is expressed. The DNA gets 'read' in a different way. Epigenetics goes against the idea that we only inherit things from our biological parents through the DNA code. Although it's still debated amongst scientists, many state that epigenetic inheritance means that a parent's experiences can be passed on in the form of epigenetic tags. Consider the impact of this for a moment. If we want to create real systemic change, there is work to be done here to heal what has been passed on through generations. The good news is that many believe that this can be reversed. The past doesn't dictate the future, but to reverse any generational gifts that aren't serving you, you have to act. Healing, understanding, acceptance and compassion are needed. Some may manage this alone, whereas for most of us, support can pave the way more easily. Therapy, EMDR and other healing mechanisms are greatly effective for many.

Mapping your reality may be a great first step towards identifying where you might want to do work. Illuminate where you may be carrying forward something that is not yours. Then go on to do the work to give it back to where it belongs in your system. This may be part of individual family work or in an organisational setting – you can use it to map teams and show any hidden dynamics or entanglements that each person may be bringing.

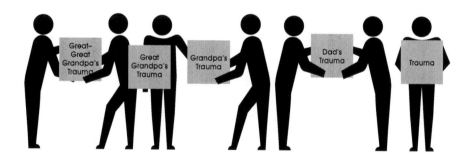

Making a change to heal generational trauma and free yourself up to make different choices sounds tricky and yet doesn't need to be. Breaking the habits that are formed due to past generations' epigenetic tags can be done relatively easily and quickly once you know what to notice and understand what is needed.

In any system, whether organisational or family, three things need to be taken care of for healthy change to occur. They are Place, Order and Cost. An example of this that I experienced recently was when a client, let's call her Jane, came to me with a coaching objective of wanting to be able to flex her leadership style and be able to motivate the younger members of her team. As we explored the topic, the rational approach wasn't bringing any insight, so we stepped into a more fully embodied mapping of the situation using her intuition and felt experience of what was happening (see the constellations section of this book for more on this technique). As we did so, it emerged that in her family system, there was a grandmother who had been experienced by all as terrifying. She had ruled the family through quiet fury and, with few words, had been the one to make all decisions. We noticed that because of her impact on the family, she was never talked of or remembered. She was treated as if she did not belong and therefore didn't have a place in the family system held for her. At this point, a penny dropped for Jane in her understanding of the resistance she felt whenever she had a young person in the team who needed support. She had learned that the only way to be with younger generations was to rule through fear. This didn't fit with her value set or leadership style more broadly, and so was making her 'stall' and unable to step into a space of relationship with them. The grandmother needed to be given her place, Jane needed to re-member her and give her back membership to the family system. In doing so, this released so much tension and opened up new possibilities for how she could now lead in her organisation.

This story clearly shows the power that comes from allowing everything that should belong to have its place. We need to consider and attend to place or belonging, the principle that everything has its place and that anything that is missing or excluded will continue to make its presence known until given its place. If we don't, then our behaviours are impacted, and we can become stuck in a pattern that is not ours.

Behind every action is a positive intention

A bold statement, you may think, and it is certainly one that is difficult to hold when you consider some of the atrocities that happen in the world today. As we explore this thinking, I believe it is helpful to remember that no matter the framing and context, you can observe the positive intention without condoning the behaviour or impact. It is helpful to separate the behaviour from the purpose and therefore be able to accept that for the person exhibiting the behaviour, good or bad, there is a positive intent behind it. For example, it may be that the person who is acting in an aggressive way towards you is coming from a place of self-protection. Now this in itself doesn't mean it is okay that they are being aggressive, but it can inform the action you take to change the situation. If self-protection is the thing that is needed, then reassurance that all will be okay is much more likely to calm the person and stop the aggression than either responding in defiance or joining them in the aggression will. This can be true for all humans and is especially true when working with something like a neurodivergent or autistic meltdown.

Not so long ago on a family trip to my homeland of Cornwall, we stopped for dinner on the way. After dinner, our ADHDer and autistic son had it stuck in his mind that he needed to get a specific football top to be able to watch a match when we arrived. It's useful to mention here that in his world, once something is in his mind, then getting to completion is the only moment that he can let go of the anxiety. So as we left the food hall, he saw a sports shop up on the trading estate. I agreed to walk up with him, knowing that as it was 8pm, the likelihood was that the store would be closed. I set him up to know this was a possibility and that if that was the case, then, as a backup plan, we could head into Truro the following day and sort things out. The store was closed, but the B&M next door clearly wasn't and he made his way in. At this point, my husband arrived in the car and we agreed that getting something from the store as a distraction was a way to alleviate the impulsivity that comes with ADHD. After a 30-minute wander up and down every single aisle in the store, he made his choice, we paid and then went to leave. Unfortunately, the store setup meant you could easily flow straight back into the beginning of the store again, which is what our son chose to do. By this time, it was 8.45pm, and we still had nearly two hours to drive, so my impatience was bubbling under the surface. At this point, our son went into a full-on autistic meltdown, throwing things in the store, threatening to steal things and then running out into the car park where he proceeded to kick the car and begin to hit my husband. To keep him safe, we were holding him and trying to keep him from running within a small area of the car park. This approach seemed to add fuel to the fire. We took a breath and remembered that all behaviour is communication, and behind it there is a positive intent. His aggression was telling us he felt out of control, that his emotions had got too big for him to manage, and he wanted everyone and everything to go away. We had no access to a quiet, dark room, but we were able to continually say, 'It will all be okay, we will keep you safe', and to reconfirm out loud for him that he was more in control than he thought he was. We were going nowhere, and he was safe. It took the best part of an hour, and the wonderful manager of the B&M looked after our unlocked and open-doored car as we ran with our son to release the cortisol and things began to calm. (It turned out the manager had two autistic children at home so knew what was needed.) Without the holding of the belief that behind every act is a positive intention, we would have continued to increase pressure, and the aggression would have built.

Consider for a moment what happens in your workplace when a behaviour that you don't want to happen occurs. What approach do you take? Do you react to the behaviour or do you consider the communication behind it? Are you noticing the positive intention that the person will be running and creating your response based on that or potentially adding fuel to the fire by reacting to the symptom?

The next time you are faced with a behaviour that needs to change, allow yourself to pause and wonder where it may be coming from before you act. Notice the label you are giving the behaviour as the label will be directing your reaction. You may find that your response then creates the shift much more easily and quickly than you could ever have imagined.

Reframing thoughts

Negative characterisation	Positive reframe
Bossy	Good director, natural leader
Compulsive	Efficient, attention to detail
Dramatic	Emotionally aware, expressive
Demanding	Assertive
Messy	Practising skills, learning
Sensitive	Intuitive, aware of feelings
Unfocused	An abstract thinker, processing information

Natural hierarchies take precedence in times of change

Even in small organisations there will be a hierarchy. Anywhere there are groups of people, a 'pecking order' will emerge – sometimes informally and at other times explicitly in the form of an organisational chart. Even where an organisational chart exists, the natural hierarchy remains. Power isn't always dictated by the level at which you sit in a structure.

In psychology, hierarchy is thought of as a clear ordering of individuals on some behavioural dimension, such as dominance-submission. When you add in the premise of social dominance theory, which argues that all human societies form group-based hierarchies, our current struggles to create more gender equity are no surprise. A social hierarchy where some individuals receive greater prestige, power or wealth than others will inevitably have 'rules' that are set up to keep those with the power at the highest level within the system. It is going to take a systemic approach that works with the natural hierarchy to create significant and sustainable change; otherwise, we risk reinventing and reinforcing what is.

Organisational hierarchy can be a useful way of creating layers that provide clarity in day-to-day working. It is in times of change that the natural hierarchy takes over. This often means that those with longer service or the bigger network are the ones who truly affect the direction of the organisation and not those in the top seat. It's what many of us will have experienced when a new process or system is implemented in a company. It's clear what is needed – often, training and support are provided, but the thing falls over anyway. If those who are at the top of the natural hierarchy do not buy into or believe in the change, the pecking order kicks in to sabotage it. Understanding where influence lies beyond the organisation chart and structures is the key to making things move and happen. Without it, you will hit brick walls or find things simply not happening, often without a clear reason why. Find those with personal influence rather than positional power and include them in creating steps to develop an inclusive culture. This way, you have given a voice to those who can be the difference between a sustainable change happening and stalling.

VUCA times

Does volatility, uncertainty, complexity and ambiguity (VUCA) sound familiar? Even before the global pandemic, many industries and areas of business would have defined their context as constantly changing, volatile and uncertain. The idea of being able to set a course to hit goals and then simply work hard to get there on the path is one for the history books. The complexities that exist and the uncertainties created are real and need navigating with a flexibility of leadership and action like never before. With this as a backdrop, we need to be mindful and acknowledge that the natural hierarchy has the lead. It may be the senior leadership who set the strategy, but when it comes to making it operationally possible, it's those with the unnamed but known power who are running the show. This is a useful phenomenon to tap into where you want to change cultures. The only failure is in not noticing or working with what in reality is happening in the system. If you only focus on seniority, then you will trip up. Flexibility, adaptability and agility are the name of the game in a VUCA world. To thrive, individuals need to be responsive, flexible and adaptive. Traditional approaches and change management techniques aren't the most effective in these times. Embracing difference to ensure the very flexibility of thought and action that is needed to succeed is what you get when you create inclusive environments where all brains, bodies and beliefs can have a voice.

Tips on how to thrive in a VUCA world

1. Lean on difference, and develop spaces that overtly call on diverse thinking and lived experiences.

2. Develop resilience – learn how to adapt and overcome situations like adversity, change, loss and risk.

3. Focus on what you want – reframe your thinking from surviving to thriving.

4. Hone your agility when it comes to learning – grow your ability to figure out what is needed when you find yourself in a different situation.

You'll notice that all of these tips become more possible where you embrace difference – that's why it's tip number 1. If you can tap into a network of people whose lives require you to have the ability to think creatively, be resilient and bounce back in the face of adversity, you've made the perfect start. Sitting in an echo chamber of sameness does not work in a VUCA world.

Elders' wisdom

Somewhere along the way, Western society has lost the value of tapping into our elders' wisdom. The fountain of youth has become all-encompassing and held in the highest esteem. Now, I believe, is the time to redress this balance and lean into what has come before as the truest resource for facing the uncertainties of the future. Learning from past mistakes, going slow to go fast, sitting with our discomforts and allowing solutions to emerge rather than forcing the pace – all outside of the norm and of great value. Wisdom is born of experience and endurance. This cannot happen without time. It is not that there is no value in youth, as that is often where energy and enthusiasm to act comes from, but to take this without the resources provided by the wisdom of our elders is foolish. While wisdom can be accessed at any age, it is usually best expressed once you have moved out of the heat of the emotion and moved through and out of the emotional reactions to other people or situations. With age comes the ability to step back and notice the whole context for many. When you notice the whole, you are better placed to make sure that all are included and that the flow of life is maintained rather than entangled.

Order in any system, be it family, organisation or society, is key to the ease, forward motion and flourishing of life. There is a specific order in the system and a need for predictability. The most common and classic order that's considered is chronological age, which within a family system makes sense as it is very clear who came first. However, even in this seemingly obvious setup, entanglements occur because human beings have egos, and some have a tendency to make themselves 'bigger' than others, irrespective of order. This often leads to slowed progress and a lack of being able to move on or away from a situation. It leads to resistance and defence from those who rightfully did come first. As the youngest of three in my family of origin, I often find myself in a space where I need to tread carefully. Being significantly younger and more tech-savvy than my siblings or parents puts me in the position where, on every trip to visit, I am greeted with a pile of post and questions that need working through, with topics ranging from finding pension pots through to disability allowance claims. It would be really easy for me to step into the 'grown ups'', place as the person doing the organising, having the conversations with agencies and sorting out claim forms. If I were to do so, though, I would be taking away the strength and choices from the owners of the issue or challenge (my brother, sister and mum in this case). They came first, so I need to treat them with a sense of support and encouragement to utilise their own agency in terms of what they want to happen. In organisational systems, it is common to see the overtaking of those who came first, and this can be the cause of major rifts or project failures. To attempt to take the place of the 'elder' or the person who has the historical references is churlish at best and disrespectful at worst. Organisational systems also have orders around things like seniority, expertise and level of contribution to the overall success of the organisation to take into account. This leads to greater complexity in many ways, and in practical terms means we must pay attention to the flow of the hierarchy – both natural and structural – to make significant change stick. The point is that orders can be felt in organisations and can give information about what still needs to be recognised for the system to function well.

Exercise: Creating 'right-sizing'

When we think about 'right-sizing', it's useful to remember that the archetype of helping is that of parent to child, and so to truly impact a system and create change, we need to first check in with ourselves as to who it is we are really helping. Are we stepping into parental helping mode so we feel better ourselves? Often, being helpful actually weakens the person who is on the receiving end of the help. The person doing the helping is stepping in to feel bigger, better or more clever, or they are uncomfortable with the current situation and want it to stop.

One way of ensuring that you are strengthening rather than weakening, and therefore creating the circumstances for lasting change, is to aim for 'right-sizing'.

Here's one way how:

1. Set yourself and the person/people in chairs opposite each other. This can be done literally or in your imagination, depending on the circumstance.

2. Harvest what it feels like for each person from their place.

3. Imagine first placing your ancestors behind you – your parents, your grandparents and so on – remembering that without your biological parents, you would not be here.

4. Imagine placing the other person's/people's ancestors behind them, and notice what happens.

Including others' parents behind them in your inner map helps us to remember the right order of things – that we are human and facing another human. It enables the seeing of a different perception. Ancestral patterns exist in our DNA and are unconscious. To include them in your mind's eye often can be, at the very least, grounding and, at best, the way of uncovering hidden patterns so you know where to target and make change happen within the system or individual.

'Walk like you have three thousand ancestors walking behind you.'

Unknown

Patriarchy and the female fight

Fighting the patriarchy is more than talking about equal pay. It's about combating everyday subtle sexism and establishing support for each other through both men and women in the workplace. It's about smashing the system, the patriarchy itself, and not each other. Both men and women are victims of the patriarchal society that we live in. It crosses gender lines and sets us up for internalising messages that hold back women. It's time to break the cycle for the good of all. Any system that does not want women or girls to be angry, ambitious, profane, attention-seeking, lustful or powerful is one that is stacking the odds against women getting to the top of their field. To have to limit your emotional scope based on your gender is a nonsense, and yet it is something that lives and breathes. Just last week, I was at a client's, and I joined in the style of conversation that was happening in the room, which included profanities (I admit to loving a good swear in the right places). One of the senior managers leant over to me and told me that every time I swore, a little part of him died. Nothing said to the men, just me – really subtle, I know, and a blunt attempt at putting me in my 'place' as the only woman in the room. Had I not been alert to what was happening, it could easily have stopped me from contributing, as it was an underhanded put-down.

> 'If you ask most people, especially men, "What is patriarchy?", It's like asking a fish, "What is water?"'
>
> **Mona Eltahawy**

Historical norms

Understanding historical norms and the roots of our language and beliefs at a societal level really matters. Often, the subtle put-downs are not even noticed as the language is based on old stories that have been left in place as an echo of the past when women were known to be less than men. As an example, just think about the word 'hysterical' for a moment. When is it most commonly used, and where did it come from? The root of the word is from the Greek *hystera* or womb, so it can be no surprise that through the ages it has been applied most commonly to describe a woman who is emotional and thought to have lost control, and never as a positive. In fact, many 'hysterical' women were placed in asylums in the 1800s to early 1900s here in the UK. Showing emotion that didn't fit the norm of the time was seen as a mental illness. Without knowing this, you may still consider it an acceptable use of language. When you consider what it is upholding as being okay in society – that women must only behave a particular way, and if they don't they will be put down or ridiculed – then it has to be one to drop from your vocabulary. An exception, of course, being for 'hysterical laughter', which is most definitely gender neutral.

It's important to be aware of historical ripples and to understand the norms that we have come from.

Let's have a look at careers, education, household responsibilities and marriage as well as prevailing stereotypes for the 19th century and then allow yourself to make a comparison to the world that you grew up in and live in today. What's changed?

To me, the changes that have been made highlight why the different phases of feminism that brought them about are to be honoured, from the suffragette movement through to the bra-burning feminists of the 1960s and beyond to today.

	19th Century	
	Women	Men
Careers	Middle- and upper-class women generally stayed at home, although if educated (not the norm) then they could be governesses or school teachers up until they married. Lower- and working-class women had jobs outside the home, including domestic servant, farm worker, prostitute, seamstress, factory worker or washerwoman. Some started work as young as eight years old and all jobs were lower paid than men's.	Many men laboured all day. When an upper-class man had the same job as a middle-class man, he was treated with greater respect. Men formed literary societies, scientific labour organisations, reform groups, sports leagues and other professional bodies. Men had higher wages.
Education	Very few women were educated, and it was not encouraged for them. If a woman wanted to go to school, it was frowned upon. Women did not have the privilege of going to college. Upper-class women were 'allowed' to be educated, but it couldn't interfere with their household responsibilities.	Men received a higher education than women, with middle-class boys going to grammar schools and upper-class men going to universities. Public schools put a great emphasis on character building through sports.

	19th Century	
	Women	Men
Household responsibilities/ marriage	95% of women remained at home. All inheritances would belong to their husband upon marriage, as the husband had rights to everything the woman had. Women were usually married in their early to mid-twenties and were expected to stay at home and look after the children and the home while the men earned the income.	Husbands were expected to provide for their entire family. Husbands dominated family decisions. Fathers didn't have an active role in their children's lives. The Matrimonial Causes Act of 1857 gave men (and only men) the right to divorce on the grounds of adultery. Then, once divorced, because the children were the man's property, he could deny the mother access.
Stereotypes	Women were expected to be mothers and housekeepers (and workers, depending on class). Their sole purpose was to find a husband, have babies and spend their lives in service. They were known to be weak, dependent, domestic and illogical. Women were completely controlled by men.	Common expectations of men: They could not show emotion or any mental/ physical weakness. They had to be strong, wise and forceful and exhibit an aura of aggression, daring and violence alongside toughness, confidence and self-reliance. Men needed to have a good status and success.

After noticing the shifts when you make your comparisons to the now, allow yourself to think to the next century. If you were compiling a table for 2100 and beyond, what would you be putting into the boxes? What would you be proud for future generations to be reading? Raising our awareness of our ideals when it comes to career, education, household responsibilities and the prevailing stereotypes means we are much more likely to get there. Where attention goes, energy flows. It takes a whole heap of energy to shift the lens, and shifting the systemic societal lens is at the heart of the change needed to make a real difference. Although I am focusing on gender here, if one shift happens, then a ripple effect will occur. Opening our minds and hearts to embracing difference in one realm means the mindset is there for the inclusion of all who may be perceived as different. Then the world changes – for the better!

Lived experience trumps theory

You can only understand what is really happening in the world when you slow down and truly listen – not to the media's version of events or to the streamed social media messaging through algorithms, but to actual people. Ask questions, be curious and prepare yourself to be able to hear some truths that may make you feel uncomfortable and even shock you. Much of the messaging that you hear oscillates between telling stories that would have you believe that equality exists and those headline grabbers that show you where it still doesn't. Now, both are true in some ways, as many of us are now able to live much fuller lives with greater choice than previous generations. At the same time, it is still the truth that women are paid 9.4% less than men for doing the same job (the same since 2017),[6] that fewer than a third of UN member states have ever had a woman leader,[7] and that those with a neurodivergence make up an estimated 50% of those entering prison compared to only 20% of the general population.[8]

Creating relationships and a psychologically safe environment for lived experiences to be shared is a starting point for us to be able to hear the truth of what is happening around us. The bigger-picture shift can feel overwhelming and simply too large for each of us as individuals to influence. We can make a difference in our own spaces, though, and the voices of one can become the power of the many. So consider for a moment where you might go to begin to understand others' lived experiences. Where can you have influence to make changes? What could you personally be doing to break stereotypes, challenge the current norms and make it acceptable and encouraged for people to come and be themselves. Once you have asked the questions, pause and allow yourself to really imagine what that feels like for the person walking that path. Then ask what they would like to be different. Do not assume that they want you to fix it for them. Often, the person who has the experience of being excluded or treated unjustly has a deep-felt need to make things right for themselves. If you step in and 'make things better', you are often putting them into a helpless position and making yourself the big hero. Now, if you are a leader in the environment where the injustice is happening, there may well be structural changes you can make to mitigate and change the patterns of behaviour. It could be that there are specific individual circumstances that require immediate action, depending on the severity of what you hear. And respecting the wishes of those who are having the lived experience, who have been courageous enough to open up and share them with you, is of paramount importance, or you may just be pushing them into a victim space.

It's important to remember that understanding the theory and background of cultures and exclusion is a good first step. Only a first step, though. The place to make lasting change happen is in the conversations and interactions you have in the real world, not in the studies and theories.

The unheard voices

Embracing difference requires all voices to be heard. It is one thing to invite the marginalised into the conversation, another for them to feel able to speak, and yet another for them to actually be heard. One of the key ways that we can learn to create equity is by learning to listen to the unheard voices and to recognise the struggles of the marginalised. In a systemic sense, anything that should be included must be for things to be in balance. Without balance, nothing can run smoothly or for a long time. I often picture the image of a baby's mobile above their cot. If you take one of the characters off the mobile, it will no longer sit in balance and do its job of entertaining or relaxing the child. Without the marginalised voices included, the mobile of life is out of balance and won't work either. The marginalised may need more than us simply recognising or listening out for them. They may not be audible. We all 'speak' in different ways. In everyday life, I have the gift of being reminded of this fact. It has been a gift in so many ways to have the opportunity to raise our son. His way of being in the world as an autistic ADHDer has opened up a world that, as a neurotypical person, I did not even know existed. There are times when his brain and nervous system have got so full in terms of sensory input that his only method of communication is non-verbal or grunting. Noticing energy levels and types of energy means that, as parents, we are better able to meet his needs on a daily basis to help him grow up into the man that he was born to be. This ability maps across and out into our interactions in the workplace and beyond. Once you can feel a need as well as see or hear it, you are better able to spot opportunities to enable equity to happen and the unheard voices to be part of the conversation.

Unheard voices may have been silenced for so long that they are barely audible or, in many cases, not speaking at all. We must be listening with our hearts as well as our ears to be able to get the full picture of need. The unheard voices are critical to this understanding, and from a place of privilege, whether racial, economic, gender, or religious, we simply cannot see the full picture without listening for the unheard voices. When creating any system, process or way of working, we need to be people-centric, not task-focused. That way, we make sure the efficiencies are built in a way that serves the many and is adaptable.

To ensure we are not perpetrating the very injustice that I speak of, we must begin by earning the right to be an ally for each and every unheard voice by first listening. Then we advocate for them in their voice – not our own, as this makes them 'lesser than'. Our role is then to strengthen and amplify their voice of self-advocacy so that it resounds throughout society.

> '"I believe we can change the world if we start listening to one another again." I still believe this. I still believe that if we turn to one another, if we begin talking with each other - especially with those we call a stranger or an enemy - then this world can reverse its darkening direction and change for the good.'
>
> **Margaret Wheatley**

Peer groups and echo chambers

The people we spend most of our time with are a reflection of who we are in the world. The peers we choose affect our beliefs about what is possible, both for ourselves and the broader world. The standards of your peer group quickly become your standards. I see this most clearly in certain teams I work with around organisational cultural change. One particular example comes to mind where a new general manager came to a site where I had been working as a coach in a global corporate culture change programme. This particular site had a history of really low employee engagement survey results, and the commercial and customer feedback results mirrored these, as you would rightly imagine. Dave, the new general manager, understood that to get the commercials into a healthier place, he had to look for ways that would enable his team to turn things around and then offer great customer service. He realised that the peer groups within his team of 200 people had, over time, set very low standards. These standards were an exact match for the way they themselves were being treated. The staff kitchen had cupboard doors hanging off, the rear stairwell that connected the shop floor with the facilities didn't even have lightbulbs, apart from the emergency exit, and one of the ladies loos didn't have a seat! The previous manager hadn't been a nasty or uncaring person, but he had purely focused on the bottom line, which had then created a peer mentality that every action had to save costs. Dave decided that he needed to do something symbolic to show the team the standards that he now expected. He called in maintenance crews over one weekend and had the place redecorated and the staff kitchen replaced, and he brought in a team of trainers to provide a refresh on what great customer care really looked like. They sat as a team and agreed how they would be together from this point onwards and how they would call each other out if they fell into old habits like shouting across customer areas to each other. By taking these actions and holding the standards, Dave had set the tone, but the difference that made the difference was what the team did next. They picked up the baton and fully embodied the new way of working. Anyone who didn't fit with the new culture and who continued to moan, gossip and generally shrug in a mindset of 'This won't ever work' soon realised that the team weren't colluding anymore. Over a three-month period, 20 per cent of the team moved on to other organisations without one person being fired. They all self-assessed and realised that they no longer fitted with the peer group standards. A key to creating this was that the leader was explicit about expectations – he demonstrated what he said both in his own behaviour and in what he set up for the team. He showed that if he treated the team as really valued people with whom he wanted to spend time, then they would treat customers the same way.

The power of the echo chamber cannot be overlooked, and it is easy to find yourself unconsciously building a peer group of people who look like and think like you do. In the example above, the approach used confirmation bias for positive good as it was done consciously. Neurotypical brains are wired for confirmation bias, which is a tendency to favour information that reinforces our existing beliefs. If we have a peer group that is made up of people who are similar to ourselves in terms of characteristics like race, religion, sexual orientation or economics, we are likely to repeatedly encounter information or opinions that reflect and reinforce our own. Do a self-check right now. Write down the names of the ten people that you spend most time with. Now write down their race, gender, sexuality, neurotype, etc. What do you notice? Have you inadvertently created your own echo chamber?

Echo chambers can be tricky to recognise, especially if you are part of them. If you're ever wondering if a particular social group, online space or team that you are part of may be an echo chamber, stop and think through these questions:

1. Do you/they tend to give only one perspective on an issue?

2. How much of the viewpoint is supported by evidence? Or is the evidence incomplete or pure rumour?

3. Are facts brushed past, explained away or ignored whenever they go against that viewpoint?

4. If your answer is yes to any of these, then you may well have found yourself an echo chamber.

For us to make more inclusive environments and to develop broader thinking and better decision-making, we need to break down these chambers once we find them. There is no single easy way to do this, but there are things we can build into our routine ways of working and living that may well give us a greater chance of being able to embrace difference.

Tips to avoid echo chambers

- Check multiple news sources so that you make sure you are getting complete and objective info.

- Remember that just because you want something to be true, it doesn't make it a fact – opinions and facts are different, and confirmation bias is a real thing.

- Interact with people of different backgrounds who have differing perspectives. Take the time to discuss new ideas with facts, patience, acceptance and compassion.

- Be aware that your online experience will be affected by algorithms, and you will be in a filter bubble.

Exercise: Network mapping

When thinking about our peer groups and network, it can be really helpful to draw a map of who is in your current network with enough detail to be able to notice differences or homogeneity. You can use any method of mapping that suits you, from Post-it notes to mind maps. Here's an example to help get you started:

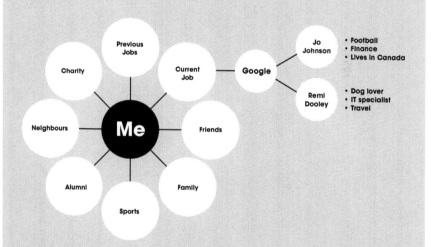

Once you have created your map, allow yourself to notice where the gaps are in terms of diversity. Now the work begins. Consider ways to connect with those you aren't currently speaking with. Prioritise your first-level contacts, as they are likely to be the ones you are most comfortable reaching out to. Share with them your desire to broaden your network and to expand things in a way that you can get to hear different perspectives and views. Ask who they know who might be interested in having a conversation and connecting. Keep track of your progress and celebrate as it grows, knowing that the wider the breadth of contacts, the better your decisions and view of the world will be.

CHAPTER 5

Do your own work first

Any journey has to start at home. Wherever that home may be, the journey to equity, inclusion and embracing difference is the same. We must begin by working on ourselves, proactively working on our own bias and how we use our privileges while applying acceptance and compassion to ourselves as we go. The changes needed often run deep, as this isn't simply about academically learning or even experientially grasping a new skill. This takes courage, it takes a willingness to be vulnerable, and it takes tenacity.

We all have bias

To judge is to be human. It's a way that we sort the world and decide what's in it as far as we are concerned. To me, though, there is a marked difference between making a judgement and being judgemental. A life without judgement, although potentially blissful, would be without depth or discernment. A life without being judgemental, though, can be one where we utilise our energies for positive good rather than damning deeds and words.

To have bias is a perfectly normal thing, so let's first state that really clearly. To be biased does not make you a bad person. A bias is a tendency, trend, inclination, feeling or opinion towards or against something or someone. Navigating life without bias would be pretty tricky, to say the least. Most of us have a lifetime of conditioning from schools, religious institutions, families and the media, to name a few, so it is unlikely that anyone can be a clean sheet and unbiased. First impressions happen. They are often based on stereotypes, and we need to train ourselves to be critically reflective on our judgements and to raise awareness of our blind spots.

The unconscious and conscious brain

Where bias becomes a problem is when it is either on autopilot and therefore running unconsciously or where the bias leads knowingly to preconceived and unfair outcomes due to personal opinions.

The first step for all of us in this is to acknowledge that we do have bias. Then we can go on an exploration of self-observation to notice what they might be. Ask trusted friends to share any they may experience or that might pop up that you could miss. Most of all, though, allow yourself to be open to the possibility that some may be of a nature that you don't like. When you find them, catch yourself and make a conscious choice to make a change. That may include needing others' viewpoints and perspectives, and it will need you to raise your awareness. Understanding the cognitive biases can enable us to notice things more readily and cut ourselves some slack to then change things, rather than wasting energy beating ourselves up or feeling guilty. Cognitive biases are repeated patterns of thinking that can lead to inaccurate or unreasonable conclusions. They can be really helpful in some circumstances as they may help us make quick decisions, but they are not always accurate, so it is important to be aware of them and attempt to counter their effects whenever possible.

In service of raising awareness, here are a few of the most common biases that we run:

Confirmation bias – This is where our brains have a tendency to sort in information that supports what we already believe and ignore anything that may go against that, despite its relevance.

Anchoring bias – This is where we jump at the first piece of information that comes our way and use it to 'anchor' our decision-making process from that point. We do this unconsciously and without checking the accuracy of the information. It could be incorrect or prejudiced and will therefore skew our judgement from the get-go.

Hindsight bias – This is a psychological phenomenon that allows people to convince themselves after the event that they accurately predicted it before it happened. Often you'll hear a few different versions of this: 'I said that would happen' is a memory distortion; 'It had to happen' is an inevitability tendency; and 'I knew it would happen' is foreseeability.

The halo (or horns) effect – This is where your first impression of someone colours how you perceive them overall. If you consider someone to be beautiful, you are likely to assume other positive traits and say things like: 'Whenever they are part of the team, positive things happen. They are so wise.' If your first impression is negative, for instance if they are late or unkind in some way, then you assume the worst about them across the board: 'How could they be smart/brave when they just said something so bluntly?'

Other mental functions to have an awareness of are the heuristics of availability and representativeness, as they are habits that can lead us down paths that do not end at an equitable place.

Availability bias – This is a tendency to use information that comes to mind quickly and easily when making decisions. For example, if asked which was more deadly – a great white shark or a Catherine wheel firework, then many people would say shark, of course. This is because we've heard many more stories in the media of people dying from shark attacks than fireworks on bonfire night. It is wholly inaccurate, though, as the odds of getting attacked and killed by a shark are 1 in 3,748,067, and you are more likely to die from fireworks, with odds of 1 in 340,733. In a work context, this plays out, as in many organisations there's a common belief that women in their thirties stop working in order to start families. However, a global survey by the ICEDR found that men and women around the age of 30 were leaving work at the same rates and for the same reason – to work for a competitor. So nothing to do with starting a family at all!

The availability bias is increasingly impactful and common now that the use of social media is so prevalent. We no longer await the 10 o'clock news to hear what's been happening in the world as we are constantly drip-fed data throughout the day, be it via news app alerts on our phones, TikTok, or through comments from friends on Instagram or Facebook. My advice here is to check your filters and always double-check facts before reposting or sharing data received this way.

Representativeness or the conjunction fallacy – Amos Tversky and Daniel Kahneman are famous for their work on a large number of cognitive fallacies, including this one where they created the 'Linda the Bank Teller' illustration. For this, they asked participants to solve the following problem:

Linda is 31 years old, single, outspoken and very bright. She majored in philosophy at university. As a student, she was deeply concerned with issues of discrimination and social justice, and she also participated in anti-nuclear demonstrations. Which is more probable?

1. Linda is a bank teller.

2. Linda is a bank teller and is active in the feminist movement.

In their research, more than 80% of participants chose option 2, regardless of whether they were novice or expert statisticians. In reality, the probability of the two events occurring in conjunction is always less than or equal to the probability of either one occurring alone. The error made by the 80% is because of representativeness: the fact that Linda resembles a prototypical feminist skews our ability to predict the probability of her career.

Priming – A technique called priming is one that many of us will have seen fantastic showmen like Derren Brown use (amongst his other talents) on television shows. Individuals are primed on their journey to the studio so that when he asks questions of them he can have some certainty of their answer as he sets their brain up to filter in particular information.

So if I talk to you about food and then show you the picture on the left, you will most likely put a 'U' in the gap of the word shown below. If I were talking to you about cleaning or having a bath and showed you the picture on the right, then most likely you would put an 'A' in the gap.

The most important thing to understand about bias is that the aim isn't to abolish it. That would be impossible because our brains are wired to create these types of cognitive shortcuts. What we need to focus on is raising our bias into conscious awareness and deciding whether it's fair, equitable and in service of the outcomes we want to create.

Awareness is only the first step

Take a moment and have a little look back over your life so far. Notice the number of times you may have known something and yet acted as if you didn't! I know when I reflect, especially on my twenties, there were many moments where magical thinking took the lead, and although I knew something about a particular person, myself or a specific situation, I would dive in headlong anyway, hoping it'd work out differently. Most of us learn through life experience as well as through education.

I believe it is becoming increasingly important to look at the topic of equity and inclusion, not only through the lens of learning to lift our level of awareness and then taking different actions but also at the level of identity. Consider the levels below and notice that if changes happen at each level of depth, the resilience and sustainability of the change will be affected. We can know something and forget relatively quickly, and we can behave differently and then have old habits kick back in, but if we do the 'real' work and challenge ourselves to address our identity – who we are in this world – then the changes we make stay because they are in the muscle.

Knowing – is about content and context. What I know. My knowledge.

Doing – is about practice. What I am able to do. Skills and competencies, including how I engage and interact with others.

Being – is about identity. How I experience myself and engage in relation to the world around me.

The power of naming

The incredible thing about language is that we can bring things into existence by simply naming them. During the pandemic, I was lucky enough to be pointed in the direction of a really creative man who focused on the impact of language and other really fascinating topics that affect the human condition. At the time, I was deep-diving into having as many online, virtual training experiences as I could so that I could pull on what worked and learn from what didn't as I transferred my own workshops onto Zoom. One story that he told really stuck with me. It was about a project he did called #HBGOA – The Hungerford Bridge Gallery of Outsider Art – where he wanted to test whether he could label something into existence. The answer was a wholehearted yes, as it quickly went global without any formal marketing.

My memory of his tale goes something like this: On his regular commute across the walking bridge that connects the South Bank by Waterloo Station and the north side of the River Thames by Embankment, he saw on one of the pillars a sleeping bag and a couple of pieces of rubbish hooked between the spikes that were there to deter pigeons. It got him thinking about what makes something art, or even a gallery. So he experimented, and the next day he came back with a sign saying 'Hungerford Bridge Gallery' and a couple of his own pieces of art. What happened next was unreal, as social media went bonkers. Millions of people were posting photos of the 'gallery' and sharing it around the world. He named it, and it became what he said it was – a really impactful example of the power of naming in my view.

So consider for a moment what you give names to. What labels do you apply to people, teams, your environment or even yourself? Are they set to make you stronger or the interactions positive and going towards what you want as an outcome, or are they bringing something into existence that is counter to your goals? Of course, it is important to know that just by naming a person a genius or a team as creative, that doesn't make it true. We need to back up naming with education, intention and action. The one thing that can be counted on, though, is that no matter how much education, intention and action you take, if you name something in a way that is contrary to what you want, then you won't get your desired outcome. A team that needs to be creative being called the traditionalists just won't cut it. I listened to one of Simon Sinek's recent podcasts as part of preparation and research into an 'agility in decision-making' workshop, and he spoke of the impact of labels. He mentioned that calling gatherings amongst warring factions 'peace talks' may be part of the reason they so often have multiple rounds or simply fail. Talking is good, but in these situations, listening and actually hearing is arguably much more important. Talking to make your point can only take things so far and rarely into the realms of compromise. Maybe calling them 'peace-listening' spaces could be more intentional towards the actual outcome.

There are too many examples of everyday labels to list here, but here's a starting point for you to begin to notice where your biases may be leaking out or being reinforced by unhelpful naming:

'She's a *chatterbox*.'

'He was the *class clown*.'

'She's always got her head in the clouds, missing the detail – such a *daydreamer*.'

Naming the emotion we feel can be a really positive way to defuse or reduce the strength of response we have to certain labels. Our ability to name emotions comes from a relatively primitive function in the brain where we developed a range of emotional expression which was suitable for life on the savannah. Daily life for most of us, though, doesn't require facing the same range of challenges and threats we may have had on the savannah. We still have the same emotional range but may have lost the ability to express it as we recalibrated to a set of different life events. So here's the question – how many of the wonderful variety of emotional responses have you chosen to code in your brain and label? Can you, for instance, easily distinguish between joy and elation or between satisfaction and fulfilment? Do envy and jealousy get coded in the same way for you, or can you differentiate? Or discomfort from stress? By extending our emotional vocabulary, we have access to more labels that will affect our brains in a way that can reduce unwanted strong responses. We can use the labels to moderate or modify our emotional response to situations. For instance, if you only know how to feel angry, then you won't have the option of feeling a bit upset, disappointed or incandescent instead. The more options you give yourself, the more you will also be able to recognise for and with others. Noticing our emotional responses to difference or when we are on the receiving end of exclusion can mean that we are able to stay more resourceful in the moment and positively effect change.

Exercise: How to build your emotional vocabulary

The great news here is that the brain finds it difficult to tell the difference between emotional responses that are real and imagined or remembered. This means that most people have a fantastically full reservoir of emotional experiences from which they can draw.

So if you want to find out what it feels like to be triumphant, for example, follow these steps:

1. Remember a time when you felt triumphant, and if you cannot remember an actual time, then imagine what it would feel like to be triumphant. The brain will treat them the same.

2. Put in as much detail as you can. What were you seeing (or what would you see)? What were you hearing (or what would you hear)? What are you feeling (or what would you feel)?

3. As you do this, recognise and notice changes that will be happening in your body, like your heart rate, breathing, mood and posture.

By putting a label to the feeling, you are creating a new distinction in the activation patterns within your emotional system. This means that you will find it easier to access and return to this emotional state whenever you want. The more states you code and label this way, the more flexible and versatile your emotional responses will become so you will find yourself in a better position to deal with difficult and uncomfortable situations. Repeat the process as many times and as often as is useful for you, making sure to prioritise the emotions you would like to have greater access to.

Looking at the table below is one way to help yourself prioritise and notice your bias. How many of the following emotional states can you discriminate between? Notice any bias you might have between positive and negative. Pick three that you are less familiar with and that you would like to have, and then follow steps 1–3 above.

Amused	Delectable	Joyous	Pissed off	Unstoppable
Amorous	Embarrassed	Kooky	Proud	Unsavoury
Abundant	Empathetic	Lordly	Quiet	Ugly
Angry	Feminine	Litigious	Restless	Victorious
Baffled	Guarded	Manic	Righteous	Vicious
Bountiful	Gregarious	Misunderstood	Ready	Vindicated
Brilliant	Gobsmacked	Nubile	Surprised	Well
Congruent	Healthy	Overwhelmed	Tasty	Weird
Creative	Intense	Old	Timid	Youthful
Crafty	Jealous	Pathetic	Trustworthy	Zen-like

We all have different maps of the world

There are no two people on Earth who have exactly matching blueprints of how they experience and view the world. Even identical twins will have different life experiences that mean some of the biases and coding that their brains pick up and create will be different, albeit subtle in some cases. Mental maps and world views are affected by what we go through in life.

Irrespective of whether the happenings are good, bad or indifferent, they will impact on the map. Like any good hiker will tell you, though, the map is not the territory. Seeing contour lines close together on an Ordnance Survey map is not the same as feeling the burn in your muscles as you climb the hill. Seeing the pub sign on the map doesn't tell you if it's the kind of place you'd like to visit. This is important to remember, especially when we are working or living with someone whose map is not just different but in many ways incomprehensible as it is based on a wiring system and baseline understanding of the world that is so different. Neurotypical and neurodivergent brains are a great example of this. I cannot even begin to imagine what it is like for my son, or anyone with autism, to not have a brain that filters out the majority of stimuli in any given second. I can seek to understand, but I'll never know what it feels like. Just because I can research and study in the hope of empathising, much like being able to read a map and see the contour lines showing hills and ditches, until I actually visit the land I cannot know what it's truly like, and autism isn't a land I can go to. So even when we get to a place of empathy, acceptance and understanding with others' needs, we cannot fully embody them. That's why it is so important, in my view, to come from a place of curiosity and questioning, whether you are with someone who has difference or you are faced with someone who refuses to go beyond their bias and stereotypes.

Neurodiversity and experiencing exclusion

Since our son was around four or five, we have had an inkling that he had more energy and a different way of approaching the world than other children. The real moment of 'Oh, that's a challenge' was when he started at school. The comparisons that were made by others were astonishing. On reflection, much of what we experienced was pure discrimination. When the world is set up in a specific way – bias towards meeting the needs of the neurotypical – then you often find that your needs are not met with catastrophic outcomes. In our case, the school literally excluded our son for his behaviour at the age of five. They were in the process of logging evidence and making an application for an education, health and care plan at our request as they knew there were some additional needs emerging, and yet when it came to what we now know were autistic meltdowns, he was treated as if he was a naughty boy. The shock of repeatedly being called into school and the school youth worker visiting our home and suggesting reward charts and the naughty chair – both of which add to the issue for any child with ADHD and autism – was immense. The final straw came when the headteacher threatened us with legal action if there was one more incident! This is a very extreme example of exclusion in the mainstream system, but I can sadly report that it is not uncommon.

I have started by talking about how excluding the education system is for children who have neurodiversity because it is the very place where we teach the next generation how to behave and be with their peers. Outside of the home, it is where life lessons and norms are learned. So, for other young children to see a child with a disability be treated as a 'bad' child and banished from school as punishment, to have them excluded from school trips and for no one to be corrected when they talked about him as misbehaving and naughty, certainly sets a tone of what is acceptable. It's not a tone that creates the kind of world I want to live in.

The mindset is the difference that could make the difference here. This is true for parents, carers and educators alike. You can choose to come first from a place of belief that no child is bad or good, that all of their behaviours are a way of communicating and that it is our job as adults to figure out what needs are being expressed. The way you frame things really has an impact. If we had thought about our son not fitting in the school, it would have been him who was wrong. Instead, though, we held it in our minds and conversations that the school was not the right shape for our son. Our task was to find a place that was his shape and then things would work smoothly. In many ways, it's the equivalent of going from judging a fish for its ability to climb a tree to getting the fish in the water and judging them based on swimming! Being in the right place is important. Sometimes, the changes needed to make this happen have to be big, like they were in our case when we moved as a family 150 miles to get to a right-shaped school and environment for our son. In other cases, tweaks can make all the difference – things like having quiet space, a blackout tent to block sensory input, a trampoline to bounce out energy and low-demand times of day, to name just a few. The cookie-cutter way that our schools are measured drives behaviours that only fit those in the middle of the curve. With flexibility of mind, it is possible to work within the guidelines and create a space that teaches our children how to be with those who are different. It is the only way that we will sustainably shift stigmas and miseducation. Start at school. Educate the educators about things like the fact that many autistic students can be outspoken in tutorials and classrooms. In most schools currently, the tutor may consider them to be disruptive and punish them or ask them to stop attending. Given that the student will probably have difficulties with social communication, asking them to no longer attend if they cannot be quiet is most likely discriminatory and most definitely excluding. To know that it is the way the autistic brain needs to process the learning, to name it so that the class is aware that they process things differently, and to set up a flow that allows for it, would be a way of including more people, some of whom may simply be external thinkers. It's what having breakout groups as a facilitator of learning is all about. You put people into small groups to discuss and then come back together in the larger group to share ideas, learnings and questions. It's best practice in adult learning, so it surprises me that schools aren't using similar methods to accommodate different needs. Often, the adjustments that can be made to support neurodivergent needs have a positive impact for all.

Fostering neurodiversity in the workplace is something that I am noticing more, although not enough in my view. With some organisations really recognising the powerful potential of building teams of people with neurodiverse differences, it gives me hope that not only will this positively impact people like my son as they get to adulthood, but it is also what is needed to really impact the mess we seemingly have got ourselves in as a human race. Environmental, political and commercial sustainability are a few of the broken but still operating systems that, without new approaches, will most likely collapse (or explode) at some point.

The challenges that need to be addressed around miseducation and stigma are at the heart of the change that is needed. A recent report by the Institute of Leadership and Management revealed that the highest level of bias was against employees with Tourette's syndrome and ADHD. One in three (32%) businesses in the study said they would be uncomfortable employing or managing someone with either of those conditions. It was one in four (26%) for autism and dyscalculia, one in five (19%) for dyspraxia, and one in ten (10%) for dyslexia. With one in seven of the population having some form of neurodivergence, this is a massive talent pool that is being missed out upon. With so many neurodivergent people reporting feeling isolated, excluded and stereotyped, businesses are losing out on the rich contribution that they could be making, even when they have been employed. Some of the answer lies in having the right policies in place that name neurodiversity as a specific minority. Training to raise awareness is also important. However, some small changes that are grounded in daily work and life can make the biggest impact. Consider doing work trials rather than traditional interviews. Run team training that includes how neurodivergent people think, feel and behave, including examples and opportunities for new team members to share how they communicate with the wider team. Make exceptions to hot-desking policies and make sure the desk or workspace suits the individual's needs. Provide assisted technologies. Create allyships within the organisation. And above all, call it out if someone is judging a colleague based on their difference.

Personality and focus of attention

When considering how to best approach our own personal development or, for those of us in leadership roles in our lives, supporting the development of others, we need to take into account personality preferences and interests. Now, for the ADHDer, focus of attention is critical, as without interest, focus is hard won, if not impossible. Hyperfocus, in fact, occurs when an interest is piqued. No matter what time of day, if the interest or idea lands, it will swallow time and be as if time no longer exists. For those of us without this skill, following an interest is more about finding ways to motivate ourselves. Hyperfocus is a superpower that needs tapping into and supporting. Making sure the person hyperfocusing remembers to eat, drink and have rest breaks is important because these basic needs will not be met instinctively. Neurotypical with neurodivergent can be the perfect pairing to really get things done.

Assuming, because you are reading this book, that embracing difference is of interest to you, I'd like to share some thoughts and insights that could be useful in helping you to flex style and accommodate others. When it comes to our approach to the flow of life and how we operate in the world, there are two main preference types, known as 'J' and 'P' in the Myers–Briggs Type Indicator. Each preference will arguably find neurodivergent thinking styles easier than the other. Below are descriptors of Jungian-based personality preferences alongside some typical traits of autism and ADHD. Know that these are to be held lightly, as human beings are much more complex than any model or attribute might suggest. It's often said that when you have met one autistic person, you will only know the traits of one autistic person. So please use these descriptors as a useful lens to help you identify where your own stretch challenges may be in this work rather than this being the holy grail of checklists.

These are two examples of neurodivergence, and the descriptors are not all of the time for all of the people. Hold them more as possibilities to aid understanding.

Autism	ADHD
Need things to be structured	Time blindness
Prefer certainty	Live in the moment
Literal thinkers and communicators	A million ideas a minute
Ordered and methodical	Tangential thinkers and communicators

For these personality preferences, think of them a bit like handedness. Most of us have a dominant hand, be that right or left. We can also, if we practise, learn to use the opposite, but this will most likely feel uncomfortable and take effort.

J preference	P preference
Like to come to closure	Keep a range of choices available
Make plans and like to start early	Remain flexible
Act in a controlled way	Respond to emerging information
Prefer to act within a structure	Prefer to go with the flow
Prefer to schedule activities	Prefer to be spontaneous

Noticing our differences and where the stronger reactions or struggles may happen is a useful thing to bring into your awareness. When we are aware, we can notice if we go into a triggered state and make it about the difference and not the person. Different ways of being and perspectives should be approached with curiosity, acceptance and compassion to be able to gather the best outcomes. Enabling yourself to be in the most resourceful state to be able to adapt in the moment or plan for the interactions, depending on your preference and those involved, is key to success.

Without difference, the world is screwed

If we as a human race continue to do what we have always done, then we will be stuck with what we've got. If we manage to embrace changing our ways, then we can have a massive impact on the world at large. A great example of this was during the Covid-19 pandemic. When the world stopped travelling and used the local resources we had available, it had an immediate impact on the environment. Lockdown measures in response to the crisis led to a temporary 17% drop in global carbon emissions, according to a study published in the journal *Nature Climate Change*. The amount of travel that commuters do has definitely been cut due to the rise in hybrid and homeworking, but, in the main, travel has firmly come back onto everyone's agenda. Now, I'm not suggesting we need to all go back to living as if it were the 1700s and the only way around is on horseback. The negative impact on the economy and existing livelihoods, as well as people's mental health, was immense and not something we would want again. On reflection, the thing that strikes me as a great learning experience for society is to be more mindful of our choices – to allow ourselves to step off the autopilot and rethink how our economies are structured and managed. Consider regenerative approaches. The Patagonia organisation's story, as told in *Let My People Go Surfing*, for me is inspiring. The principle of not taking more from the world's resources than we are giving has to be the right balance of exchange for a sustainable and healthy future for all. To see that this can be done and a business can be commercially successful represents a blueprint I believe that we can all learn from.

During the pandemic, it was widely realised and embraced that the arts and nature enabled us to get through it. Of course, the scientists and engineers were the ones at the crisis point developing vaccines, understanding the spread of the disease and building intensive care equipment to help those with Covid survive. However, for those of us who either didn't get Covid or who managed to get well in our own homes, it was art, creative activities like music, and nature that kept us well. The number of people I saw simply out for a walk was incredible, and everyone I met felt uplifted by the air, the exercise and the change of environment.

Thinking differently and taking a new perspective worked in the crisis of it all. My hope is that as a species we can notice this and embrace neurodivergence as a perspective that is wholly needed for us to create an emerging future that will sustain.

Let's tune into what is possible and get a sense of the superpowers that we, as neurotypical folks, can tap into if only we pay attention and pause for long enough to feel the benefits. Here are some ways that the neurodiverse can help in an unusual and changing world:

1. Creativity and innovation

    •   Many successful artists, actors and entrepreneurs are neurodivergent. They have a keen sense of curiosity, imagination and seemingly endless ideas. Their unique thinking style can be harnessed by proactively giving space for their passion to come through. They enjoy talking through their ideas with others and can often find it helpful if you mind-map their ideas to help translate things into actions.

2. Resilience

- Many neurodivergent people have faced obstacles and setbacks throughout life. This leads to an ability to bounce back, to be able to 'look for the positive' and to develop strategies to help move forward. They are often those who have put in place activities and mindful spaces to manage their regulation. These practices, be they yoga, journaling, gratitude or exercise, can be mirrored to enable an earthing of the things in daily life that will nurture you and enable you to bring your best self more often.

3. Routine

- Many people on the autism spectrum have a real strength for punctuality and the cadence of how they organise their activities. Those with a neurodivergence like ADHD often have time blindness, so they may find it a struggle to relate to time in a structured or organised way and so have developed highly effective ways of coping and navigating life. These can be as small as using a phone alarm to trigger a sound to tell you when to take a break, going for a walk every morning, or having a set wardrobe to take the decision-making out of what to wear to work. (My husband wears polo shirts and shorts all year around unless it's snowing.)

4. Hyperfocus

- This kicks in for some neurodivergent people when they follow an interest. The dopamine hit is what is needed for them to find motivation, and it means they remain focused, not distracted by whatever else is going on around them, and it really boosts productivity. The downside is that time escapes them, and they may forget to attend to physical needs like food and drink, so supporting them with that can be a real help. Finding your and others' areas of interest and setting things up so you use your time on these wherever you can is a key win. Giving a role of interest in a meeting can be an easy way to keep an ADHDer engaged.

5. Empathy

- Often, those with a neurodivergence are hypersensitive to the 'vibes'. They can feel the emotions of others acutely while sometimes not being able to process or articulate the experience. This is an incredibly useful trait to have within any team environment as it means you have an early-warning system to any unmet need or even a pocket of concealed enthusiasm or excitement towards an outcome or task.

6. Honesty

- Being your authentic self and being literal are traits that are common for those with neurodivergence. Social norming doesn't get processed by their brains in the same way, so it can be freeing to be able to state their lived experience or needs. Many neurotypical people could really benefit from modelling this behaviourally, as it adds to the level of trust in a relationship, team or organisation because you know where you stand.

7. Logical thinking and problem-solving

- Those with neurodivergence like autism are typically very logical in their decision-making. This can be an incredible trait to add into the decision-making mix as it alleviates the risk of confirmation bias. When it comes to problem-solving, those with dyslexia or ADHD are often out-of-the-box thinkers with the ability to see the bigger picture. This is particularly useful in times of uncertainty and for businesses adapting to change.

Exercise: Taking a personal audit to boost the use of your superpowers

1. First, notice what your superpowers are. You may want to get some feedback from those you work with or those who know you well. Often, the things we are best at come so naturally that we don't even see them as a skill as we assume everyone can do it – a bit like breathing.

2. Once you have your list, spend a few weeks noting down when, where and with whom you use them.

3. Notice any themes that are positive and pay attention to any gaps. Where are the places, people or situations that you would like to use your superpowers but don't currently?

4. Having identified the gaps, take a moment to get into the specifics around what makes it possible for you to use your superpowers in certain circumstances. Then explore how you might build them into the gaps. For example, if you notice you use your empathy superpower mostly with your family but not at work with your team, ask yourself what's behind the behaviour. Is it that you need to know and trust people to be able to empathise? In which case, how do you connect with your team in a more intimate way to build trust? Or is it that at home you allow yourself to slow down, and at work you have your head down, powering through tasks? If so, what could you build in to allow you to pause and notice what's going on around you?

Know your impact – positional power

In any system, be it family or organisational, there are those who have power because they occupy a certain role. The power of the role will be affected by the culture of the organisation, country or family background. For instance, in a financially led market, the finance director role in an organisation may have more influence and power than, say, the marketing director, whereas in a creative industry the opposite is most likely true. The thing to notice, though, is that the more senior the role, the more your words land with impact. Leaders set the culture and tone that make certain behaviours acceptable or not. This is key if we want to shift the dial on creating truly inclusive environments and embracing difference.

Positional power in and of itself is not a problem. As my son's hero Spiderman says, 'With great power comes great responsibility', and for leaders who have this approach, true positional power can be a force for good. If, however, pulling rank is the only approach to wielding your power, then the impacts are disengagement and dread. It's important to note that this differs from personal power, which can be held at any layer within an organisation or setting. Personal power is more attitudinal and creates influence. It is a state of mind rather than an attempt to manipulate and manoeuvre or control others. It is not power that is vested in a person by others but something that we can own within ourselves, as its primary aim is self-mastery.

If you have positional power, with or without personal power, it is important to know your impact and utilise it as a platform with purpose. It's not good enough anymore to simply not be sexist or negatively judgemental of any group based on one attribute – you need to be proactive and anti-sexist. Find ways to set a tone that doesn't accept exclusionary behaviour. Make sure expectations are explicit around ways of working, behaviours and processes. Challenge yourself to notice that in any conversation, if a solution is being found for any group and you look around the table at those creating the solutions and you don't see the group being represented, then you need to stop. Any solutions created within these types of conversations or committees need to be treated with great scepticism. Get the people affected in the room into the conversation, and make sure they are heard.

We need the leaders across our world to step up and make a change. Being pro-diversity is not enough, and it doesn't automatically make you anti-sexist. If a woman has been promoted to the board, it does not mean that the boys' club doesn't exist. More than once throughout my own career, I have sat around board tables, and partway through the agenda we paused the discussion to take a comfort break. Then, 15 minutes later, when we get back around the table, the discussion has moved on. The men had been continuing the conversation in the restroom, which meant the decision was taken without female input. This is but one example of unintentional exclusion (and sometimes, let's not be naïve, they are wholly intentional). To be clear, this includes all genders and needs us all to play our part as anti-sexist. For example, not that long ago I was told about a board conversation in which they were looking at some key roles in the organisation. One director said when talking through potential candidates, 'Don't worry about her – she'll be leaving to have babies soon anyway.' Being sexist would be either saying this or agreeing with it. Being non-sexist is to walk away, say nothing or laugh nervously to cover your discomfort. To be anti-sexist, you need to act by saying something like, 'That is wrong. We need to consider her regardless,' and then follow up to make sure that happened. Remember, this isn't about what sex you are, and it's not about being awkward or offending the boys' club – it's about doing the right thing, both morally and for the organisation's success.

Challenge yourself with these questions:

1. Do I speak up when something that is 'off' or outright sexist is said, even when it is done in jest?

2. Do males and females in your organisation get paid the same for equal roles?

3. Do you ever think that a woman is better suited to office 'housekeeping'? *Notice who clears the cups at the end of the next meeting!*

4. Are you consciously making your hiring and promotion processes equitable?

5. When you talk about the culture you are creating, are you thinking about a diverse one or that people need to fit in? *(Or even that everyone you employ is someone you'd want to have a beer with.)*

6. Are you ready to be anti-sexist? *Anti-sexist definition = opposed to or intended to prevent sexism (actions based on the belief that members of one sex are less intelligent, able, etc. than members of the other sex).*

Making yourself bigger aids your survival but makes others smaller, so it perpetuates the problem

It isn't rare to experience 'help' that feels more like the helper is putting their needs first. How often have you gone to share your perspective on something or the troubles of your day with someone, and they immediately stepped in with fix-it-type solutions when all you were after was a listening ear? Those of us who care about others can find ourselves stepping into situations to help when we haven't been invited. This leads to frustration and can fracture relationships. Our drive to feel valued and to belong is strong, so in many ways it is natural for us to jump in and want to make things better for others. Unfortunately, much of the time, this disempowers the other person in a way that can only make the situation worse, even when it may fix the immediate issue.

Unhealthy helping

Unhealthy helpers or givers are often well-intended, and yet their actions belittle and disempower others. In fact, they can create codependency and do the opposite of what is intended. Unhealthy helpers can feel like they must rescue others and may tend to give beyond their energetic and material means. When we breach another person's boundary to step in and rescue without permission or invitation, we make ourselves bigger than them. In situations where other adults are in difficulty (it's different for children and those who are vulnerable), we need to first seek to understand what is best for them. When we make assumptions and do what we believe someone needs, at best we might get lucky and do the very thing they would want, but even then we have done it without their permission and so have taken away their agency. A great friend of mine shared an example of this very thing with me at a research retreat we were running recently. The story they shared was one where a member of their broader team had attended some diversity and inclusion training. This had made them realise that they wanted to become an ally to those at work who were in minority groups. Sounds good, right? Well, the intention was good, but the execution wasn't. In the next team meeting, the individual began answering questions on my friend's behalf and started speaking up for all non-white employees. Instead of creating space for her to speak, they took the role of spokesperson. This form of helping not only takes away the voice of those being marginalised or unheard but also makes the person speaking on behalf of them the hero and therefore bigger. This isn't about levelling the playing field and creating equality of voice, and it can often be a form of masking. Masked helping occurs when we can't bear the situation. We want what is happening to stop, and so we step in to rescue. We all have different tolerance levels with difficulty, and so we will often deflect by 'helping' or using humour. If either of these acts are done consciously, they can be useful, but often they are an unconscious act and get in the way. When we can stretch our window of tolerance for difficult feelings in awkward or challenging situations, we can begin to use the tension creatively to take a step towards better outcomes for all.

Bert Hellinger's Ordering Principles: The Orders of Helping

Five Orders (ordering principles)

- 'We can only give what we have. We can only take what we need.' If we are trying to help someone who does not need our help, then it is we who need help. Also, by doing this, we might rob the person of the experience.

- 'Respecting the destiny and circumstances.' We agree to the person's destiny, and we only support the person as much as the circumstances permit. Such help is very restrained, but there is strength in it.

- 'Adult to adult.' We act as adults towards the person and treat the person as an adult. This will stop any attempts of the person to bring us into the role of a parent.

- 'Less personal, more systemic.' The perception of a helper should be less personal and more systemic. Every person is part of a family system. We need to see those who are excluded in order to take the significant next step.

- 'As is.' Loving each person as they are, without judgment. Opening our hearts to them. Whatever is reconciled in our own hearts can be reconciled in the person's.

'Helping is an understanding that goes beyond, into something greater and all-embracing.'

Bert Hellinger, psychotherapist and founder of family constellations

Learning to sit with discomfort is what will change things

This may sound like something from a therapeutic setting, and in many ways it could be. I'm naming it here, though, as a practice or way of being that can enable real shifts to happen at a personal, organisational and societal level. As ever, though, this has to begin with the individual. Many of us have been taught that feelings are things to be acted upon or swept under the carpet. Within this sits the art of toxic positivity, where we are told to count our blessings or keep a gratitude journal. Now, I'm not suggesting that these cannot be good practices for training the brain to notice the positives, because they are for many of us. What concerns me, and I believe stops real systemic change from happening, is when we label some emotions as negative and therefore run the 'act or hide' programme. All emotions are simply signposts for either things that have happened in the past that haven't been dealt with yet and now need attention or for things that in this moment require attention. They are neither good nor bad. No emotion is innately negative unless it is fuelling a negative action or reaction. They simply are a signpost from your limbic system pointing you towards growth or clarity.

Sitting with uncomfortable feelings rather than reacting immediately or distracting yourself means that you can start to relate to the emotions at a deeper level. Allowing yourself to pause, feel what you feel and let yourself breathe into the discomfort so it can settle is a practice that makes deep change possible. When we act too quickly, we may temporarily feel better, but we will rarely have got to the root of the feeling or issue. The layers need time – sometimes only a moment but more often space to emerge. When it comes to creating systemic change to embrace difference, we will inevitably uncover our own biases and elements of our learned generalisations that will be uncomfortable and need to be let go of or shifted in some way to create a new way forward. Building up our tolerance for discomfort is a way to enable growth to be less painful.

Being uncomfortable is something to embrace. Putting yourself in new and unfamiliar situations will trigger your brain into a dopamine release.

Dopamine is known as the happy brain drug – it creates motivation and enables real, sustainable change.

Above-the-line and below-the-line brain states

Studies by the Conscious Leadership Group have captured some truths about our behaviours as human beings that are important to understand if you are to be part of the solution rather than the problem when it comes to creating equity. This thinking and knowledge can be applied to any situation where change is required and is a must in terms of embracing difference to change the world.

To get 'unstuck' and embrace difference, we need to be in a particular brain state.

Noticing your brain state at any given moment is the first step to being a leader in your own life. Imagine for a moment a line drawn horizontally on a page that represents what's going on in any given day. If you are above the line, you are in a brain state that is creative, open to change, curious and committed to learning. If you are below the line, then your brain is set up for protection – it is defensive, closed and committed to being right, often at all costs.

Below the line, you hold a belief that there is not enough. You live in a world of scarcity where there isn't enough money, love, time, energy, etc. Your behaviour is threat-based, and you are seeking approval, driving for control and needing a sense of security above all else. In this place, your brain tends to get you to cling to your opinions, to rationalise and justify behaviours and to gossip or blame others.

Above the line, you are creating allies and coming from a place of curiosity. You listen to differing views and opinions while questioning your beliefs. All of this happens in a playful and light way, but that is of real importance. Above the line is a way of being that knows there are difficulties but also that there are solutions. Finding what is working, knowing that solutions can be found and that every moment has change within it so 'this too shall pass' are necessary traits to be successful when things get tough.

Now, we all go below the line, and in fact our brains are hardwired to do so. If you are walking down a set of stairs and one step is broken, you are wired, literally, to notice the broken one because it is a physical threat. Think back to cavepeople – the brain was formed for survival, and so a chemical concoction was released when a threat was perceived. Back then, threats would kill you! The challenge today, though, is that our brains don't differentiate between a physical threat and a knock to the ego. When psychological safety is missing, it sends us below the line. When we are below the line, we are literally not in a brain state for connection, innovation, collaboration or creativity.

As my great friend Sally says, 'Head up, tits out and stride forwards.' So, when you notice yourself going below the line, know that you have a choice. It's not that going there is wrong, as there are times when hanging out in that place is wholly appropriate, but it's not the right place to be in terms of brain state if you want to build connection, do things differently or create sustainable change.

We must connect before we correct

Whenever we are on a quest for personal growth and behavioural change, there will inevitably be bumps in the road. We can be certain that there will be times when we get things wrong, and we may even feel like we are going backwards. In situations where others are impacted, the 'getting it wrong' isn't the thing to focus on – it's creating connection that matters first. This is true whether we are the one who made the error or if someone else has acted in a way that has negatively impacted us. To give or receive feedback (formal or informal) is only effective if you are in a relationship with the other person. Connection is key and cannot happen in the heat of the moment because our executive functioning will be offline to some degree. Think about times in your life when something has gone wrong and you've got upset, angry or deflated. When has it ever helped for someone to tell you to cheer up, not to worry, to calm down, or to start offering solutions? When we want our words and actions to help ourselves or others, we first need to sit with the reality, even when it is simply a perception or misinterpretation rather than a fact. When we can empathise and connect, we can then take a step towards correction. For children, this approach is incredibly important as it helps them learn to regulate while they begin to understand the full breadth of emotions in life, a simple example being: 'I love you – and the answer is no.' For us adults, though, I believe it is equally important to practise connection before correction because it demonstrates that a person matters. Knowing that you matter means your brain will be much more receptive to what is said. You will be able to hear it as your executive functioning will be online. You can process what's happening and make sense of things. When we can make sense of things, we can choose to change.

Trigger management

It's important in life to understand your own triggers. As we began to explore in Chapter 1, they are unconscious responses that are programmed in based on life experiences and childhood learnings. In psychology, a trigger is defined as a stimulus that causes a memory, often a painful one, to resurface. To be triggered affects your emotional state, and the person, place, thing or situation that elicits the response need not be frightening or traumatic – in fact, they may be seemingly insignificant or superficially reminiscent of an earlier occurrence. When you are aware of triggers, you can notice them with relative ease. A good indicator of being triggered is when the response that you are feeling, or on the receiving end of, is out of proportion to the actual reality of what is happening. A key step in learning to recognise your triggers involves paying attention when certain things, people or situations generate a strong emotional response. Beyond the immediate surge of emotions, you might also experience a physical reaction like your heart pounding or your stomach clenching.

For us to create environments where all are welcome and equity exists, we must be aware that there are likely to be triggers that will be set off. The trigger itself is often a very useful indicator that we are on the right track when creating change. Change is rarely comfortable, and we will be challenging ourselves to step outside of our own lived reality to be able to consider things from others' perspectives. What may seem small to us can be massive for others. Since beginning to write this book, I have discovered that I am much more present with noticing things that create an internal emotional response in me that are rarely anything to do with the intention of the other person. Clients have been sharing their own experiences to broaden my understanding too. I have noticed that many of the triggers they have shared in a work context are coming from the root of an embedded societal norm. They are often things that we watched previous generations of women live through, and although they may have changed shape slightly, they are norms that uphold today and are experienced through our own lives as well. It's almost as if we have carried a box around and we're ready to jump into it and be small as soon as specific things happen. An example that happened recently in a coaching session was when a client named Jane came to me and wanted to explore a recurring pattern she noticed where her confidence was impacted. She told me about a meeting that ended with a trusted colleague of hers sharing with her that her behaviour had made them feel like she was taking over. The colleague said that instead of it feeling like a team effort, they experienced being in the back seat for a lot of the time. When Jane explored with the colleague what specifically had caused them to feel this way, they said that although they loved her energy, they found it difficult when Jane's enthusiasm meant that when she leant into a topic, they felt that she repeated what they had just said but using different words. This feedback was offered in a light touch way, but the feeling that was underneath the message had real power. The impact shared may not even have been about Jane at all. It could be that the colleague had things going on for them that meant they didn't speak up as much as they would like, so they were deflecting the reason for them not being as big a part of the work as they would want onto Jane. It could even be that the actual issue was that they weren't communicating their points clearly.

The interesting thing that came out of our coaching conversation was that Jane's reaction was a pattern that she was now able to notice. Immediately upon hearing the feedback, she took it to heart and decided it was all her problem and that she was being too dominant. She concluded it was her job to make things easier for everyone else without considering the impact on herself. When we worked through this, Jane was able to identify many times throughout both her childhood and her working life when others had told her she was 'too much'. Her habit was then to get back in her box behaviourally. In the moment, this would make it more comfortable for those who had shared their views, but in reality it was stopping Jane from bringing her strengths to the team. Without her energy, there would be little motivation, and without her expressiveness and tangential thinking, very little would be innovated and over time she would become what she described as a worker bee rather than the powerful, empathetic leader that she is.

In life, we can never know what others' triggers are. Through the process of adopting our son, our eyes were opened to the extent of what triggers are hiding in plain sight – things that, if you don't come from the care system, you probably wouldn't even notice. Some movies and TV shows can open up big feelings and conversations. A recent example for us was when watching *Shazam!*, a kids movie about a boy from a group foster home who becomes a superhero. There is a scene where they talk about 'ageing out', and in the moment nothing happened, but later that day I noticed our son seemed anxious about something, so I gently started a conversation. He immediately asked whether he would have to leave us when he was 18. He had been worrying that in six years he'd be homeless and have no parents. Before adopting, we'd have never even realised this level of impact could happen and the anxiety that simple things can cause. When you consider how many children in the UK alone were in the care system in the 1990s, many of whom are now in leadership roles or working in organisational settings in teams, it really hits home how important it is to consider our conversations and communication.

Figure 1: Number of looked-after children at 31st March, 1968-2008

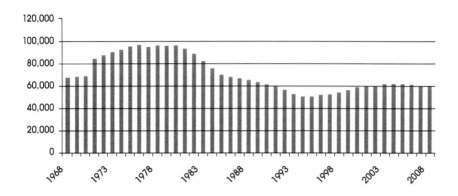

Figure 2: Number of looked-after children per 10,000 children, 1988-2008

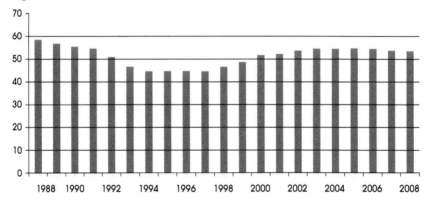

Trigger management steps:

1. Sensing – noticing in your body that you are having an emotion/feeling.

2. Naming – choosing an accurate name for the emotion/feeling.

3. Attributing – making sense of what caused the emotion/feeling to happen.

4. Evaluating – checking in about how you feel about having the emotion/feeling.

5. Acting – deciding how to cope, use or deal with the emotion/feeling.

PACE – more than one meaning

For many of us, when we hear the word 'pace', we think about speed or rate of movement. It's related to walking or an action like the progress of a building project. However, it's also a therapeutic way of parenting that was developed by Dan Hughes more than 20 years ago. This is a central part of attachment-focused family therapy to this day, and it supports adults in building safe, trusting and meaningful relationships. PACE is a way of thinking, feeling, communicating and behaving that aims to enable others to feel safe, so why would we ignore it as a way of creating psychological safety generally in life? There is so much to learn from the research and practice of this work that can enable us to embrace change and make systemic shifts that will change the world.

So what is PACE? It stands for Playfulness, Acceptance, Curiosity and Empathy. It is about how we deliver messages through our communication. In many respects, it is a way of being rather than simply a technique. Practising PACE helps us to slow down our reactions, to stay calm in the moment and to tune into what is needed. In really tricky moments, it allows us to regulate our own emotions and manage our triggers so that we can then be better able to respond to others and even help them navigate their own heightened thoughts, emotions and behaviours should it be appropriate and useful.

Research has shown that using PACE can reduce the level of conflict, defensiveness and withdrawal that tends to occur in many work and home contexts when difficulty emerges. When we are taking a defensive stance, positive outcomes for all are not possible. It is a protective barrier that can aid survival, but in times where the threat isn't a mortal danger, it is a blocker to growth and improvement. Using PACE enables us to see the strengths and positives that lie underneath more negative or challenging behaviour. It is key to remember that all behaviour is communication and that, at times, children and adults alike are lost for words. When we get to overwhelm, it is our behaviours that take over. For some that means walking away and withdrawing, and for others it may mean hitting out. Whatever our response, in these times we are communicating a need that isn't being met – not in the most effective way, and in the extreme it may be unacceptable or even illegal. If we use PACE as a way of working through the challenge, we are much more likely to create positive steps forward.

Since the pandemic, I have noticed that the use of PACE is more necessary than ever. Many more of us have had to experience first-hand mental health issues, anxiety and some level of trauma. The very absence of our normal lives and our freedoms being taken put unprecedented pressures on relationships, families and workplaces. The difficulties everyone faced with loved ones dying, jobs being lost and the inability to see friends and family have heightened our sensitivity to change. Now it is more important than ever to build meaningful connections and stronger relationships. That begins with seeking to understand and then embrace differences as we meet them.

When communicating with others, especially where things are tricky or differences are emerging, take this approach and apply the parts that feel useful:

Playfulness – Approach things with a light tone of voice, like you might do if you were storytelling. Create a fun, playful atmosphere, even when the topic is serious. Be ready to express joy while keeping rapport by matching energy. Relating to others with a playful attitude keeps things upbeat and can help diffuse a difficult or tense situation. People are more likely to respond openly when there is a touch of playfulness rather than anger or defensiveness. Having a playful stance isn't about being funny all the time or cracking jokes when things are difficult or someone is sad

– it's about helping others to experience connection and not feel alone. While this response may not be appropriate in a time when there is risky or dangerous behaviour, when you have applied it to low-level behaviours previously, you will find that it can help keep things in perspective when things get really tough.

Acceptance – This is about being in the moment and accepting that whatever you or the other person are feeling right now is okay. You need to accept the thoughts, feelings and perceptions without judgement, even when you might not agree with their interpretation of things. It is their experience, so accepting the feelings they have is different from accepting the facts. Avoid minimising or invalidating their feelings at all costs. Show them that you hear them and it is important. For example, they might say to you, 'You think I'm incompetent and can't be trusted.' It would be tempting to say, 'That's not true,' but that might make them feel unheard or misunderstood. Instead, you could respond with, 'I'm sorry you think I don't trust you and think you are incompetent. That must be awful – no wonder you're cross,' or 'I didn't realise that you felt that way. I'm sorry it feels that way to you.'

Acceptance does not mean that you have to accept the behaviour, especially if it is harmful to you or others. You need to limit these types of behaviours while understanding and accepting the motives behind them. It's all in the tone of voice. Convey acceptance by using a gentle, storytelling tone, and show interest and understanding while maintaining a non-judgemental stance. The non-verbals are what let people know what you are really feeling.

Curiosity – Be curious. Seek to understand the other person and what drives them. Find out what's important to them and strive to bring out the best in them. Practising curiosity means you don't judge too quickly because you will be asking questions and wanting to know more about them. The tone of voice here is one of quiet acceptance – questions that don't even sound like they need a response. For example, 'What do you think that was about?' or 'I wonder what…' rather than 'Why did you do that?' 'Why' questions will always bring out the defensive, and the aim here is to create a safe space so that you can connect and then correct. We need to convey that our intentions are to understand and not to lecture or reprimand.

Empathy – Empathy is about stepping into someone else's shoes to get a sense of how they are feeling. It enables us to step into compassion and is essential to someone feeling truly understood. Being empathetic isn't just about reassuring them, because that's an attempt to simply make the problem go away. It's about being with them in the moment and helping them contain and navigate the emotions and difficulties. It's a way of laying a solid foundation of connection that enables change.

With empathy, we demonstrate that we know how difficult an experience is for them and that they don't have to deal with it alone. We are in it together to get through it. When someone feels they may be abandoned at any moment within the difficulty, it will lead to more negative behaviours or a cover-up of reality. To get to real change we need to feel safe and supported as we embrace the change.

Our sense of self and others

We begin to learn about ourselves as being separate from others between six and nine months old. The circumstances around our care at this age impact how we navigate this developmental stage and how safe we believe the world to be. For those of us lucky enough to have secure rather than chaotic homes, we learn that when people leave, they come back and that our needs are met. For many, though, this cycle is one where the infant learns that when caregivers leave, they may not come back and/or their needs may not be met. At around two years old, we begin to make meaning of our sense of self, which is an integral part of social-emotional development. This sense of self is what lets us know who we are, what we like and what's important to us. As children, our sense of identity is shaped by our experiences, interactions with others, the local environment and our own unique personality. Having a strong sense of self is important when we want to be able to embrace difference. If we don't really know what we stand for ourselves, how can we connect and empathise with others' experiences?

If sense of self, self-image or self-esteem are things that you know you need to strengthen to be able to step out of your comfort zone and create systemic change by embracing difference, then there are some key things that will aid your journey:

1. Set healthy boundaries. Identify someone you know who is great at this and model them or ask them to help you learn how.

2. Practise saying no, and if no feels too harsh a place to start, then begin with a 'not right now' and build up to it.

3. Practise positive self-talk. Notice what you say to yourself about yourself and make sure that your inner cheerleader has as much say as your inner critic.

4. Travel as a way to learn more about yourself. Expanding horizons and having new experiences will show you different facets of your personality and let you know where your own 'edge' is. Being in different cultures will challenge your sense of 'norm'.

5. Increase self-awareness and decrease comparison. Pay attention to who you are and what you bring, and listen to feedback. Avoid comparing yourself to others or even earlier versions of yourself. We all do the best we can with the resources we have at any given time, so be who you are today, consciously.

6. Practise self-care. The irony here is that the very time you most need self-care is the very time that it may feel the least possible to take. So make sure to create a network of people around you that you can lean on and who will make sure you find ways to take a breath and look after you.

7. Let's get physical. Taking care of your body is a major part of taking care of yourself. Activity will only help build self-esteem if it is right for you. Find something that empowers you or that helps you let off steam. Forcing yourself to run when you aren't a runner or to swim when you hate water will have the opposite effect to what we are after here. Explore and be kind to yourself. Find something you enjoy and that helps you see your body in a positive way.

Remember that sense of self for the neurodiverse can be different. Consider for a moment that if sense of self develops and emerges through the activity in the brain in interaction with others, then if you have a brain that doesn't have a driver to interact, a sense of self may not emerge as readily. With our son, I've seen it first-hand, most noticeably from the ages of five to ten, although still now to a great extent. His way of creating a sense of identity is to notice others' preferences and try them on for size. One particular trip to the park back when he was around seven had around 12 costume changes through one football match (kickabout with jumpers as goal posts). Every time another child drew his attention, he would need to mirror them in some way. So, if they had long socks, he would need to change socks. If they were playing in a vest, he would take off his shirt, and so it went on. Today, when we watch movies, which is most nights because he finds them calming as most have been watched numerous times, he won't be able to sit and connect until he has a costume that reflects a character in the film. In a work environment, I've seen this play out where a manager has certain expectations about dress or uniform norms. They haven't been explicit about it because they see it as obvious, but for the team member it isn't understood until it is shared in a literal way, demonstrated by others and consistently upheld as a rule.

While recently working with a client who holds the role of CEO and is self-diagnosed as neurodiverse, a challenge became apparent when observing him with his executive team. The protective bubble that we all have as human beings around our bodies (called the peripersonal space) caused a misunderstanding and conflict. Some of the team reported experiencing distrust and aggression from the CEO when what I witnessed was his energy flow leaning in and being directed at individuals much closer than a neurotypical person would deem appropriate unless you were really angry. The research shows that the peripersonal space is much smaller for many with autism/ADHD than it is for neurotypical folks, and the difference between self and others is sharper. Behaviourally, this can lead to misunderstandings, and conflict is inevitable without an understanding of this. With curiosity, education to understand differences and a willingness on both sides to flex without masking, these things can be worked through. Managing our frustration with ourselves and others is often the first step to success.

> 'The mind is like water. When it's turbulent, it's difficult to see. When it's calm, everything becomes clear.'
>
> **Unknown**

Tip to stay calm when frustrated

There are many different breathing techniques that can help create calm, and this one resonates with me as it was taught to me by a friend's nine-year-old daughter. They had been learning meditation at school, and she described it as 'Smell the flower, hold the scent and then blow the petals' – beautifully simple and a lovely image as you attend to the practice. The greatest thing is that the technique is shown to positively affect the vagus nerve, so the impact is proven by science, which is wonderfully reassuring for the analytical amongst us.

Benefits of box breathing

The slow holding of breath allows CO_2 to build up in the blood. An increased blood CO_2 enhances the cardio-inhibitory response of the vagus nerve when you exhale and stimulates your parasympathetic system. This produces a calm and relaxed feeling in the mind and body. Enjoy.

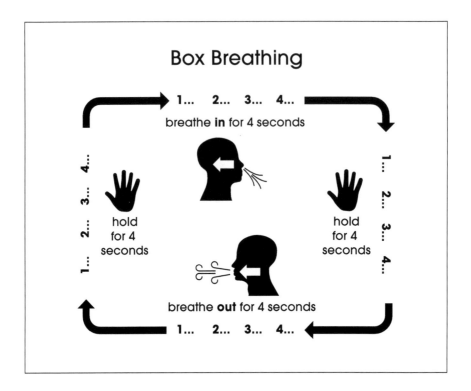

The end... and the beginning

As you come to the end of this book, I hope you have been challenged in a way that brings you and those around you growth and new insights. My hope is that you will take some of the stories, experiences and knowledge into your daily life and begin to create a positive ripple effect.

Each of us has the ability to change the world, and my belief is that if more of us can come from a place of wanting to leave it better than we found it, then the human race may well just thrive.

If in some small way this book is an enabler to creating greater inclusion in the world, then I am forever grateful. Inclusion creates trust, belonging, happiness, bonding and even better engagement and productivity, so who wouldn't want a bit of that?

What can be more important than feeling valued for who you are? Let's all strive together to not only find spaces and places where this is true for ourselves but also to make sure that in whatever environments we find ourselves, we act in a way that makes others feel welcome exactly the way they are.

We all share the responsibility to make those around us feel welcome, valued and accepted. Creating a world where we can all find belonging and bring our best selves comes through day-to-day interactions. The first step may well be the creation or change in a company or government policy, but at best that is just the beginning. It's how we are with each other that counts and that has the biggest impact.

In all of this, remember that diversity is a structural fact and inclusion is a choice we make, so it is within our control and the sphere of influence in our lives. We have choice! We can push ourselves to choose to embrace difference and not simply tolerate it. When we do, we are all set to truly make a positive change in this world.

So until next time... be kind, be curious and be brave. Love Sarah x

ABOUT THE AUTHOR

Sarah is a Cornish woman who has landed back in the West Country in recent years via the south coast and 14 years as a Londoner. She lives with her husband, son and two Bengal cats on a farm near Frome and loves returning home to her beloved Cornwall to get that much-needed blast of Atlantic air that clears the mind and refreshes the soul.

Sarah is an ICF accredited embodied systemic coach, a facilitator and a writer with a zeal for elevating performance to the next level for individuals, teams and organisations through developing inclusive leadership. She is known for her pragmatic approach to the psychology of change and her ability to connect with each client's context from a place of true understanding. Clients have said that she has a knack for getting to the root cause of challenges and asking just the right questions to unlock answers.

Her coaching practice specialises in executive and team coaching, talent management and the neuroscience of behavioural change. Over the past ten years, she has focused on her passion for bringing diversity to leadership, specifically within the space of neurodiversity, inclusion and gender equity, all with the goal of achieving high performance.

Her drive to understand others, make a difference and help people bring their whole selves to work and life has always shone through. Having worked her way up from the shop floor to senior roles in some large organisations, she stepped out on her own 17 years ago and has never looked back.

Sarah's clients range from marketing creatives to chief financial officers. Organisations she has supported include the Fairtrade Foundation, Ford Motor Company, Michael Kors, Teenage Cancer Trust, Stonegate Group, the Co-op, MSi Choices (international and UK), Battersea Cats and Dogs Home, the Royal British Legion and Cambridge Consultants, amongst many others.

For information about speaking engagements, workshops, training programmes and coaching, please get in touch. My contact details are:

Sarah Lane
Coaching Lane Ltd
The Bristol Office
2nd floor
5 High Street
Westbury-on-Trym
Bristol
BS9 3BY

sarah@coachinglane.com
www.coachinglane.com
www.equitychangelab.co.uk

ENDNOTES

1   The vagus nerve's job is to send information from your gut to your brain. Finding ways to calm this nerve through breath is linked to dealing with stress, anxiety and fear. These signals enable you to recover from stressful and scary situations. New situations are, to differing degrees, both stressful and scary, depending on your experiences of life so far. To change your internal dialogue and be able to embrace difference is very much linked to your ability to sit with feelings of discomfort and manage your state to be calmer.

2   'Looked-after children' refers to those who are currently or who have previously been in the care system.

3   The latest Women in the Workplace report was based on data from more than 300 organisations with more than 12 million employees combined. The report found that for every woman at a director level who got promoted in 2021, two women directors left the company.

4   'Progress on the sustainable development goals: The gender snapshot 2022', UN Women Data Hub. Available at: https://data.unwomen.org/publications/progress-sustainable-development-goals-gender-snapshot-2022 (Accessed: 13 March 2024).

5   'Number of autistic people in Mental Health Hospitals: Latest data' (2022), National Autistic Society. Available at: https://www.autism.org.uk/what-we-do/news/autistic-people-in-mental-health-hospitals (Accessed: 14 March 2024).

6   Duncan, P., Garcia, C.A., and Jolly, J. (2023), 'Women still paid less than men at four out of five employers in Great Britain', *The Guardian*. Available at: https://www.theguardian.com/world/2023/apr/05/women-paid-less-than-men-four-out-of-five-employers-uk-gender-pay-gap (Accessed: 13 March 2024).

7   Clancy, L., and Austin, S. (2023), 'Fewer than a third of UN member states have ever had a woman leader', Pew Research Center. Available at: https://www.pewresearch.org/short-reads/2023/03/28/women-leaders-around-the-world/ (Accessed: 13 March 2024).

8   Çokdeğerli, M. (2023a), 'Overlooked and overwhelmed: The impact of early neurodiversity screening in prisons', National Autistic Society. Available at: https://www.autism.org.uk/advice-and-guidance/professional-practice/overlooked-and-overwhelmed-the-impact-of-early-neu#:~:text=Findings%20suggest%20the%20prevalence%20of,prison%20regime%20(Criminal%20Justice%20Joint (Accessed: 13 March 2024).

Printed in Great Britain
by Amazon

44146284R00121